Windows on the Gospel
STORIES AND REFLECTIONS

Windows on the Gospel
STORIES AND REFLECTIONS

Flor McCarthy

DOMINCIAN PUBLICATIONS

TWENTY-THIRD PUBLICATIONS

First published (1992) by
Dominican Publications
42 Parnell Square
Dublin 1
and
Twenty-Third Publications
P. O. Box 180
Mystic CT 06355

ISBN
1-871552-24-9 (Dominican Publications)
0-89622-545-3 (Twenty-Third Publications)

COVER DESIGN
Banahan McManus

Printed in the United States

ACKNOWLEDGEMENTS
Cover illustration: From 'The Beatitudes' by Evie Hone.
Biblical quotations are from The Jerusalem Bible © Darton, Longman and
Todd Ltd and Doubleday and Company Inc.

Contents

Throughout the text, the headings of stories appear in **bold** type.

Introduction

Once upon a time a group of children came upon an old castle hidden in the depths of a wood. Immediately their curiosity flared up and they found themselves drawn to it as if by a magnet. On reaching it they didn't immediately head for the main entrance. Instead they started to circle the outer walls, peering in through the narrow windows wherever they could reach them.

These windows provided them with mere glimpses of the interior of the castle. But even these glimpses convinced them that the castle was filled with wonder and mystery. Their curiosity had now reached such a pitch that no power on earth could have prevented them from going inside. Meanwhile, they had lost all interest in the outer world. Completely shorn of wonder, it now seemed utterly ordinary and commonplace. For them, it had ceased to exist. Everything that attracted them was in there in the depths of this old castle.

Finally they tackled the main door which, to their delight, gave way before their combined assault, and so they found themselves in a strange and awesome world. They spent several hours exploring this world, hours filled with surprises and the odd scare here and there. Eventually they had explored it all, or at least as much as was accessible to them, and someone suggested that it was time to go home.

They were on the point of saying a reluctant goodbye to this enchanting world when one of them by chance looked out through one of the upstairs windows at the world from which they had come, the old familiar world of everyday. He suddenly gave a shout to the others, and soon they were all busy looking out from these curious windows.

They were amazed at what they saw out there. When viewed from in here, their old world looked so different. In fact, it seemed to have been transformed. It was strange, bright, and exciting.

So when they finally left the castle they came out into their old world with a sense of exitement. It was almost as if they were setting foot in it for the very first time .

When you are looking into the heart of the Gospel you feel that you are looking into the depths of life. The Gospel puts you in touch with the essence of life. No matter how often you hear its great stories told, you are continually surprised by their richness. There are so many approaches one can adopt, so many ways of looking at them, that their capacity to surprise, delight, and challenge seems endless. However, in order to experience this, you have to approach them with the openness, curiosity, and sense of wonder of children exploring an old castle.

Having looked into the heart of the Gospel, we have to return to the ordinary, humdrum world of everyday. However, having been into the castle we no longer see this world in the same way. It is now bathed in a new light. Transformed by vision of the Gospel, it is now cloaked in wonder and mystery.

In this collection of stories and reflections I do not claim to take the reader on a guided tour of the heart of the Gospel. I see it as providing so many, little windows through which. one can catch glimpses of some of the riches the Gospel contains. It is not a systematic treatise. It dips in here and there. Still, it follows the broad outline of the story. Practically all the parables are touched on and most of the familiar characters appear.

The approach adopted is a very human one. The aim is to go as far as one can on a human level. I don't believe that this excludes the element of mystery. Mystery contains the known as well as the unknown. To explain is not to explain away. To try to understand is not to deny the mystery.

The way to the divine is to follow the human as far as we can. We can never hope to reach the infinite. All we can do is to follow the finite. in as many directions as possible.

There are things which are known and things which are unknown. In between there are doors.' William Blake

If we wish to understand the gospel we have to bring to it all we know and have learned about life from our own experience and from listening to others and observing them. We should also bring to it the insights gathered from our reading. Many good books have helped me to understand and appreciate the richness contained in the Gospel. The quotations which are scattered liberally throughout the book bear testimony to this fact. These quotations also provide the names of some of the authors whose books have helped me in my explorations of the Gospel.

I hope that the book will be useful to, and enjoyed by, all those who are searching for a spirituality based on the Gospel. I hope that it will also prove useful to preachers and teachers.

Flor McCarthy

*There is something of Rembrandt in the Gospel,
or something of the Gospel in Rembrandt.*

Vincent Van Gogh

The Giver Who Began by Asking

Stephen was only two years old when his father died, and he was reared entirely by his hard-working mother. From his earliest years he set his heart on becoming a shoemaker. He worked hard at school, served his time under an exacting master, and lo! he was a shoemaker.

The first thing he wanted to do was repay his mother for all the sacrifices she had made on his behalf. He opened a little workshop but things didn't work out. He got no work, with the result that he began to doubt his ability as a shoemaker. Then his mother died suddenly. This came as a terrible blow to his already sagging morale. In a fit of depression, he threw his tools into a box, closed the shop, and took to begging.

One day he was sitting in the market place with the other beggars when the King appeared, accompanied by the mayor and other notables. One of the mayor's assistants began to tell the beggars to move on. Suddenly the king's eye fell on Stephen, who was clearly younger than the others. He came over to him and said:

'What's your name?'

'Stephen, your majesty,' he answered.

'How old are you, Stephen?'

'Twenty-one, your majesty.'

'How long have you been begging?'

'Three years, your majesty.'

'What were you before you took to begging?'

'I was a shoemaker, your majesty. At least I trained as a shoemaker.'

'And what happened?'

'Nobody would give me any work to do.'

'I see,' said the king thoughtfully. He paused, leaving Stephen wondering what was to come next, but even in his wildest dreams he couldn't have guessed.

'Stephen, I'd like you to do me a favour,' the king resumed. 'I'd

like you to make me a pair of winter boots, size nine. Do you think
you could manage it?'

'I'll try, your majesty.'

'Good!' said the king. 'How much time do you need?'

'Two weeks, your majesty,' Stephen answered.

'Well then, you've got two weeks. Now you'll need leather and
other materials. Go to Mr Harwick, the merchant. Tell him I sent
you, and he will give you what you need.'

With that the king left him. Stephen went straight home. The first
thing he did was to inspect his shoemaker's tools which by some
miracle of providence he still possessed. He was horrified to find
them covered with rust. He spent the rest of that day cleaning and
polishing them. Early next morning he went to see Mr Harwick.
Everything he needed was waiting for him.

The story began to circulate that the king had asked a beggarman
to make him a pair of shoes. At first people didn't believe it. But
slowly it emerged that it was true. Some people thought it was the
most marvellous thing they had ever heard. But others took a different view.

'The king was just trying to be nice to the old beggarman. He'll
never wear those boots,' said a shoemaker.

'I think it was mean of the king,' a leather merchant claimed. 'After all, he's a very wealthy man. The least he might have done was to
give the beggarman a little money.'

But those who took an unfavourable view of the king's action
showed they knew little about their king, and even less about the secret of giving.

Meanwhile Stephen was at his workbench. He was delighted to
discover that he had lost none of his old skills. Each day he started at
dawn, and worked late into the night. Yet he experienced neither
ache nor pain. He took no chances, and cut no corners. He lavished
his undivided attention on the smallest detail of the work. Every
hole he made with the awl, every stitch he made with the needle,

every tap he gave with the hammer, was executed with the utmost care and precision. The boots began to grow in his hands..

He finished them with a day to spare. They were magnificent. Many people came to see them. All who did so were amazed that a beggarman could do such splendid work. On the appointed day the king's messenger arrived to collect the boots. A week went by. It was an agonising week for Stephen. He didn't know what to do with himself. He walked the streets for hours, and sat for ages on park benches. But he did not beg.

Then on the eighth day the messenger came back with the news that the king had tried the boots on and found them a perfect fit. By way of thanks he gave Stephen a scroll, bearing the royal seal, to hang in his workshop. In the scroll the king said he was happy to know that in his kingdom there was at least one craftsman, who not only knew his trade, but put his whole heart into it.

Stephen never did go back begging. From that day on he had more work than he could cope with. And what really endeared him to his river of customers was the fact that he gave all, rich and poor alike, the royal treatment.

• • •

Often in the Gospel we find that Jesus begins by asking something from the very people who come to him in need. For instance, he asked the Samaritan woman for a drink. He asked the servants at Cana for pots of water. He asked the disciples for food in the desert. There is surely a message here.

It is always easier to do things for other people than to help them find their human dignity and self-respect by doing things for themselves. The greatest good we can do for others is not to give them of our riches but to help them discover their own.

> I lived on the shady side of the
> road and watched my neighbours'
> gardens across the way revelling

In the sunshine.

I felt I was poor and from door
to door went my hunger.

The more they gave me from
their careless abundance the
more I became aware of my beggar's bowl.

Till one morning I awoke from my sleep
at the sudden opening of my door and
you came and asked for alms.

In despair I broke open the lid of my chest and
was startled into finding my own wealth.

Rabindranath Tagore

'*What nourishes one's heart is not what one gets from the wheat, but what one gives to it.*' Antoine de Saint Exupery

'*Live not by what you receive but by what you give; that alone augments you.*' Antoine de Saint Exupery

'*Those who ask nothing of you, do not constrain you to be.*' Antoine de Saint Exupery

Thirst
John 4:1-30

In olden days wells were great meeting places. It wasn't only those who were thirsting for water who went there. Many a lonely soul, thirsting for a chat, also went there.

But the day Jesus arrived at the well in Samaria he knew exactly what he wanted. It wasn't chat. It was water. His throat was dry and his tongue hard. He looked into the well. What he desperately needed was down there in abundance. But without a bucket there was no way he could get it. He had no choice but to wait until someone came along.

Finally along came a Samaritan woman, a bucket dangling by her side. Jesus watched as she lowered the bucket into the well and brought it up overflowing with clear, sparkling water.

'Give me a drink,' he asked.

The request surprised her. Nevertheless, without hesitation, she placed the bucket in front of him. He sank his head in it and took a long drink. When he finally raised his head she said, 'You were thirsty.'

'I was, but now, thanks to you, I'm okay,' he answered. Then he added, 'But you are thirsty too.'

'That's why I've come to this well,' she replied.

'I'm not talking about that kind of thirst. I'm talking about another kind of thirst.'

'I don't know what you mean,' she said.

'I think you do,' he said gently.

With that she began to reflect on her life. She was deeply unhappy, and had been for many years. Inside her she felt an ache, a pain, a longing. Yes, she thought, it's like a thirst. It is a kind of thirst. She wondered how this man whom she had never laid eyes on before seemed to understand her better than she understood herself.

'I guess you're right,' she said finally. 'I am thirsty.'

'Have you ever tried to quench your thirst?' he asked.

'Yes, many times. I've been married seven times.'

'And the thirst is still there?'

'Yes,' she replied, 'and it's getting worse.'

'The first thing one has to do is identify the nature of this thirst,' he continued.

'I feel so empty,' she said.

'What you're experiencing is an inner thirst – a thirst of the heart and the spirit. But you're not the only one to experience this thirst.

Everybody experiences it.'

'Everybody?'

'Yes, everybody.'

'Everybody!' she repeated as if talking to herself. 'And I was beginning to think that there was something wrong with me. How does one satisfy this thirst?'

'Only with the kind of water God gives,' he answered.

'What do I have to do to earn this water?'

'Nothing. It is a gift – a gift which God gives to his thirsty children,' he replied. He paused, then added, 'But I also can give it to you.'

'Really?'

'Yes.'

'Please give me some of this water so that I'll never have to come to draw water from this well again.'

'You don't understand. You are still thinking in terms of ordinary water. Whoever drinks ordinary water will get thirsty again. But whoever drinks the water God gives will never know thirst again. It will be as if he had an eternal spring inside him.'

'Well then, give me some of this other water.'

'You've already got it.'

'But how can that be since I'm thirsty?'

'The spring is there, and has been all along. It's just that it's been out of your reach, just as the well-water was out of my reach until you came along with your bucket.'

They chatted for some time more. Finally she said, 'Thank you.' And with that she departed.

Even though he hadn't given her anything, as she went away she was feeling differently about herself. Something was beginning to happen inside her, something mysterious but very real. It was like something awakening, like the bubbling up of a spring, a spring of new life and new being.

Marvellous things happen when people begin to awaken to the

gifts God has placed within them.

At this point the apostles arrived back and the woman fled back to the village. There she invited all she met to come out and meet a man who 'has told me the whole story of my life'.

Of course, by 'whole story' she didn't mean her complete biography. You sometimes hear people say, 'One failure after another,' or 'One disappointment after another – that's the story of my life.' So what the woman was saying was: 'Here is someone who knows exactly what my life has been like. He has pinpointed my problem. He really understands me.'

To feel understood is the beginning of salvation.

'Only the pure of heart forgive the thirst that leads to dead water.' Kahlil Gibran

The Day of the Lord's Favour
Luke 4:16-30

In the synagogue at Nazareth, Jesus announced that the long-awaited 'Day of the Lord' had come at last. The blind would see, prisoners would be set free, the down-trodden would be liberated, the poor would have the good news preached to them, and there would be a year of favour from the Lord for everyone.

It was an incredible announcement. Yet it was not received as good news by everyone. How come? The cancellation of debts is wonderful news for debters, but not so wonderful for bankers. The announcement of a coming feast is great news for the starving, but no big deal for the well-fed.

For people such as the Pharisees, the Day of the Lord was to be the day when the elect would be separated, once and for all, from the non-elect. It would be a day of the Lord's judgement. And here was Jesus declaring that it was a day of the Lord's favour, not just for the deserving, but for everyone. It was more than their narrow hearts were capable of accomodating. Yet Jesus announced the good news courageously and joyfully, even though he knew it would provoke a hostile reaction from the self-righteous.

The Tenants

The kingdom of heaven is like the case of a landlord whose tenants fell into arrears with the rent. Having once fallen behind, things went from bad to worse. Pretty soon they found themselves entangled in a web of squalor and debt. Seeing no way out of their predicament, they lost heart and hope.

Now the landlord was a kind and patient man. Even so, the tenants wondered how much time he would give them to pay up. The awful thing was that even if he gave them till doomsday, they would not be able to do so. Recently they had seen the new chief bailiff making his rounds, so they figured the day of reckoning was not far off.

During his rounds, the bailiff naturally asked each one how much he owed. But surprisingly he went far beyond this. He insisted on going into their homes, enquiring about what they ate, about the sick and the disabled, the young and the old. In fact, he wanted to know about all their problems and worries.

Then one day he sent out word that he wanted to see all the tenants. He had a very important message from the landlord for them. So the long-awaited and much-dreaded day of reckoning had finally arrived! The tenants assembled in fear and trepidation.

When they had assembled, the bailiff mounted a makeshift platform. The tenants knew, or thought they did, the speech he was about to deliver. Indeed, there was scarcely a person among them who couldn't have written it.

'In the course of my rounds I have discovered that every single one of you is in debt, many of you up to your eyes. Now I know that times haven't been easy, and the climate hasn't always been kind.

Nevertheless, at the end of the day you've no one to blame for your situation but yourselves. You're a bunch of foolish, lazy, good-for-nothings. The landlord is fed up with you. He has been very patient and very understanding. He has given you not one chance but umpteen chances, and still you have failed to come up with the goods. He was hoping that it wouldn't have to come to this. But you have left him with no other option. He is taking the land away from you forthwith and giving it to others who will pay their rent.'

This is what they were expecting him to say, though in their heart of hearts they were longing for something else. Before beginning, the bailiff let his eyes roam over the assembled tenants. He noticed the anxiety on their already deeply-furrowed faces. Then he began to speak.

'The landlord has asked me to deliver the following message to you. He knows that all of you have run into debt, many of you very deeply.' He paused. They waited for the blow to fall, and braced themselves against it. 'Well,' he resumed, 'I've got good news for you, very good news.' Again he paused.

Good news! They couldn't believe what they were hearing. They opened their hearts to receive it like fledglings opening their mouths to receive food from their mother. 'The landlord has asked me to tell you that you can forget about your debts. He is wiping the slate clean. From this day you can start all over again.'

Shouts of joy went up. The tenants embraced one another. Some began to dance and sing, things they hadn't done for a long time. As they made their way home with light hearts, they noticed for the first time in years that the sun was shining, birds were singing, and fragrant flowers were blooming in the fields.

'God's grace is infinite. It demands nothing from us but that we await it with confidence and acknowledge it with gratitude.' Karen Blixen

The Call to Repentance

Jesus began his public mission with a call to repentance. 'Repent, and believe the Good News.' (Mark 1:15). To answer the call to repentance one must feel a kind of dissatisfaction with oneself, and have a longing for something better. There must be a sense that something is wrong, a feeling that something is missing.

The conversion experience begins with the sowing of a seed, a mustard seed perhaps, but one which can germinate and bear fruit in time. What is this seed? It is the realisation, however vaguely glimpsed, that we are not what we could and should be. This realisation is the first step of a journey, the first stage of a process.

To take on board the call to repentance demands openness, honesty, humility, and above all courage – the courage to put an end to self-deception, and confront a painful reality. People can become so set in their ways, so sunk in ruts, that it becomes close to impossible to move them. It's almost as if they were set in concrete. Still, it's not that they can't be moved, but that they won't be moved. People can get so used to being dressed in rags, and feel so comfortable in them, that even if you gave them a new suit of clothes for nothing they wouldn't wear it.

Such people can glimpse, or even see clearly, a better future, and still they won't move. They realise that this future can't be achieved in the twinkling of an eye by means of some magic wand. They realise that the road forward (or back, as the case may be) will be long, and the progress slow, difficult, and painful. The present self can't dwell in the house of the future – it has to be a transformed self. This is why they opt to stay where they are and as they are.

The hardest people of all to convert, however, are the good, because they don't see any need of conversion. It's hard enough to get people who are sick, and who know it, to go and see a doctor. But try getting those who are sick, but who are convinced they are well, to go! But then the 'good' can't hear the Good News either. It is only

the poor, the sick, the blind, the lame, the imprisoned, sinners ...
who long for the good news and who receive it with joy.

*'Before a man needs redemption things must go ill for him. He
must have experienced sorrow and disappointment, bitterness and
despair. The waters must rise up to his neck.'* Hermann Hesse

*'Satisfaction with our lot is not consistent with the intentions of
God and with our nature. It is our duty to aim at change, at improve-
ment, at perfection. It is our duty to be discontented.'* Ralph Waldo
Emerson

*'The realisation of our greater selves comes through the recogni-
tion of what we are not. We are beggars always to what we were
meant to be.'* Laurens van der Post

• • •

At this stage in my life, if you wish to improve me, there's little
point in warning me or threatening me. I've had enough of these in
my younger days.

Instead, show me what I'm missing out on, or lacking, in order
that my life might be deeper, richer, and more authentic; then you
disturb me, and I may be moved to take whatever action is necessary. This approach makes me feel that I'm being offered a gift.

If all this sounds selfish, then so be it.

• • •

To be converted is not to become a new and strange person. In every
conversion there is continuity and discontinuity. Negative elements
are overcome, new goals are set. Our talents and gifts are not denied
but redirected. Conversion is not a demeaning thing, or a putting
down of oneself. Rather, it is an opening of oneself to one's full possibilities. This means it is something essentially positive, and invari-
ably leads to joy.

Some people respond to the call of conversion immediately. All
that is needed is a flash of insight, a moment of enlightenment or
awakening. This suggests that there is such a thing as being ripe for

conversion.

When the dissatisfaction has grown to such a point as to be painful, when one is tired of travelling down wrong paths, when one is tired of eating fruit that fails to nourish, then one is ripe for conversion, and answers with alacrity the call to the true and authentic.

'The new is only the seed of the old.' Ralph Waldo Emerson

'Desire not to change a man into something other than he is.' Antoine de Saint Exupery

• • •

Times of change and renewal, are times of great vulnerability. The most vulnerable time in the life of a crab is during the time of seasonal change – when it has just shed its old shell but has not yet acquired a new one. The converse is also true. Times of vulnerability offer opportunities for change and renewal.

'Moments of renewal are also moment of extreme peril.' Laurens van der Post

'All that is changing its condition travails and suffers.' Antoine de Saint Exupery

'No one has ever undergone a change of heart without suffering.' Antoine de Saint Exupery

Ripe for the Call

As Jesus was walking on he saw Levi the son of Alpaeus, sitting by the customs house, and he said to him, 'Follow me'. And he got up and followed him. (Mark 2:14).

He got up and followed him. – just like that! It seems unreal. Yet, on reflection, we can see how it could happen. Some people are just sitting on the touchline of life – waiting for the call to something worthwhile. If the right person comes along, with the right call, then they are up and away. They have been secretly longing for it. Life has prepared them for it as hunger prepares a person for a banquet. We begin to understand what people mean when they say, 'I did not choose it, it chose me.'

To give things to people before they are ripe for them is a waste. Worse, it may turn them off for good. There is a moment of readiness or ripeness. We can't see what we are not ready to see, or hear what we are not ready to hear. To be unready or unripe is to be unable to respond properly.

Levi obviously was ready for the call of Jesus. It seemed as if his whole life had been leading him to this one time and this one place. He was like one of those alpine flowers which, when the spring sun comes along, blooms immediately because it has been growing in secret under the crust of snow, and is only waiting for the door to be opened to burst out.

It is obvious also that he had arrived at a stage where the life he had been leading up to this had no more sustenance to give him. Christ didn't appear to give him any choice in the matter. Of course he did. He didn't order him. He invited him. But for Levi that invitation had the force of an order. Sometimes even when people are ready to take the plunge, they need a nudge.

'Sometimes having no choice is an advantage.' Primo Levi

'God screens us from premature ideas. Our eyes are screened so that we cannot see things that stare us in the face, until that hour arrives when the mind is ripened; then we behold them, and the time when we saw them not is like a dream.' Ralph Waldo Emerson

'When destiny comes to a man from within, from his innermost being, it makes him strong, it makes him a god.' Hermann Hesse

'The future has to enter into us long before it happens.' Rainer Maria Rilke

Beatitudes

Blessed are the patient – they will get things done and done well.

Blessed are the faithful – they will be like safe anchors in a world of broken moorings.

Blessed are the honest – they will be to society what leaven is to bread.

Blessed are the humble – they will find rest for their souls.

Blessed are the generous – they will keep alive our faith in the essential goodness of people.

Blessed are the caring – they will shine out like beacons in a world darkened by indifference.

Blessed are the genuine – they will glow like gems in a world of falseness.

Blessed are those who do not give up hope – they will see their dreams come true.

Looking to Nature

Blessed is the tree which takes time to sink deep roots – it shows us what we have to do in order to withstand the storm.

Blessed is the seed which falls on good soil and so produces a rich harvest – it shows us what happens when we hear the word of God and act on it.

Blessed is the vine which, having been pruned, becomes all the more fruitful – it shows us the benefit of self-denial.

Blessed are the flowers of the field – their beauty bears witness to God's prodigal artistry.

Blessed are the ubiquitous sparrows – their carefree attitude to life gives us a lesson in trust in Providence.

Blessed is the wind, which comes from we know not where, to set sails moving and breathe life into dying fires – it reminds us of the mysterious workings of the Holy Spirit.

Blessed is the sun which bestowes its light and warmth on bad people as well as good, and the rain which falls without favour on all fields – in them we see a reflection of God's indiscriminate love for his children.

Blessed are the leaves which know when to let go, and do so ablaze with colour – they show us how to die.

From the Gospel

Blessed are those who realise that they cannot live on bread alone but need the word of God too – they will be fully nourished.

Blessed are those who remember that the things which corrupt us are not those which enter us but those which come out of us, and who strive after purity of heart – they will be clean all over.

Blessed are those who, when they have sinned, follow the example of the prodigal son, and come back home to seek reconciliation – they will cause heaven to ring with joy.

Blessed are those who stop to bind up the wounds of today's roadside wounded, pouring in the oil of compassion and the wine of hope – they are the Good Samaritans of today.

Blessed are those generous doers who, in the midst of all their work, maintain a lonely place in their lives for prayer, reflection, and relaxation – they will not suffer burn-out.

Blessed are those who remove the plank from their own eyes before telling their brother to remove the splinter from his – their efforts at reforming others will bear fruit.

Blessed are those who, having put their hand to the plough, refuse to look back – they will be found worthy of the kingdom.

Blessed are those disciples who rememnber that they are the branches without which the vine cannot bear fruit – through their good works the Vine will bear the grapes of love.

Unconditional Love

Right from our earliest years many of us had the following lesson drummed into us by parents, teachers, and others: 'If you're good, I'll love you; if you're bad, I'll punish you.' It is not surprising then that we tend to expect the same kind of treatment from God. We believe that God will love us only if we are good.

But the Gospel declares: 'Your Father in heaven causes his sun to rise on bad men as well as good, and his rain to fall on honest and dishonest men alike.' (Matthew 5:45) This means that God loves us regardless of whether or not we are worthy of such love. God loves us, not because we are good, but because God is good. Our very existence is a sign of God's love. God's unconditional love for us is the Good News.

Consider spring. See how it acts towards the trees. See how faithfully it comes, and how impartially it bestowes its blessings on big ones and little ones alike. It does not wait for them to don their leaves before coming. Rather, it is as a result of its coming that they don those leaves. It comes to release them from the cruel grip of winter so that they can blossom and grow. And see how enthusiastically they respond. All but the dead obey and are transformed as a result.

Now if spring is so generous towards the trees, how much more generous God is towards us who are his children. Therefore, we do not have to worry about trying to earn his love. All we have to do is open ourselves to receive it.

Then maybe we will begin to love others as God loves us. We will not wait to discover good qualities in them before loving them. We will love them without preconditions, and then discover reasons that make them worthy of our love.

'Not till the sun excludes you do I exclude you.' Walt Whitman

• • •

At the end of a lifetime. devoted to teaching boys in a New York high school, a Jesuit priest said: 'Every boy I ever taught was infected with the subconscious conviction that if he didn't succeed he wouldn't be loved.'

Treasure in Fragile Vessels

Once, long, long ago, there was a father who had four children. When they were old enough to leave home, as a sign of his love for them, he decided to give each of them a treasure. The treasure was sealed in a simple jar made of earthenware. This surprised them. However, none of them objected. A treasure was still a treasure. So, taking it gingerly into their hands, they went out into the world.

Justin, the oldest of the four, bore the treasure away with great joy. However, the joy soon wore off. He got tired of having to handle the jar as if it were a piece of rare china. He began to grumble against his father, saying that it was unfair, even cruel, of him to ask him to carry the treasure in such a perishable container.

And yet there were times when he could see reasons for this. Was his Father not showing the greatest possible trust in him? If he had put the treasure in an unbreakable container that would not be showing much trust in him. Nevertheless, he grew tired and careless. Eventually the inevitable happened. He let the jar fall. It was badly cracked, so he put it aside. Ever afterwards he nursed a grudge against his father.

Anne, the second oldest, went at once and had the jar encased in a metal container. Then she proceeded to encrust the case with precious stones. Every penny she earned, and she earned a great amount, went into this. But she was very proud of the jar, which now glittered with diamonds and rubies, and availed of every opportunity to show it off in public. However, the result was that the new container, or rather, the outer one, became her real treasure, and she forgot about the inner treasure.

Brendan, the third oldest, carried the treasure with care and love for a while. But then he began to have doubts about its value. 'How can be sure that I'm not being deceived?' he asked himself. 'Perhaps this is some kind of joke on father's part? What if there is no treasure in the jar after all?' Falling on hard times, he sold it for a pittance, but afterwards felt guilty for having done so.

Sarah, the youngest of the four, carried the treasure with the utmost care. She had no doubts about its value, so great was her trust in her father. Even though many misfortunes befell her, she never lost heart. She had one real anchor in her life. Not so much the treasure, as the love of her father which the treasure symbolised.

Years went by. Then one day a message came saying that their father was dying and wished to see them. They figured that he wanted them to give an account of what they had done with the treasures he had given them. Justin and Brendan were apprehensive about the encounter. Anne was looking forward to it. Sarah was overcome with sorrow at the prospect of her father's death.

When the meeting took place the father enquired earnestly about the well-being of each of his children. Not as much as a word about the treasures! Finally Anne plucked up courage and said, 'Dad, aren't you going to ask us about the treasures?'

'I've already done so,' he replied.

'I don't understand,' said she.

'Why, you are my treasures,' said he.

Lonely Places

In the morning, long before dawn, he got up and left the house, and went off to a lonely place and prayed there. (Mark 1:35)

Isn't God everywhere?

Once there was a man who had a habit of going off by himself into a remote wood. One day a friend, curious to know what he was up to, followed him into the wood. When he caught up with him he found him sitting quietly on a log.

'What are you doing?' he asked the man.

'I'm praying,' came the reply.

'But why come to this remote spot to pray?'

'Because I feel close to God here.'

'But isn't God to be found everywhere, and isn't God the same everywhere?'

'God is, but I am not.'

• • •

We can find God and pray to God anywhere and everywhere – in the kitchen, in the classroom, in the workshop, in the street. Still, it is not a bad idea to have a special place to which we can withdraw from time to time – the shore, the park, the mountains, the church, or wherever.

In such places God somehow seems to be nearer and more friendly. The whole atmosphere seems to be pervaded with the divine presence. God speaks to us in the wind, in the sound of a stream, in the song of a bird, in the beauty of a wild flower, in the very silence.

And in such places we are different too. We are calmer, quieter, more relaxed, and are thus more open to what God is offering us at all times and in all places.

The Shore

It's twilight and I'm on the shore. Earlier today this beach was crowded with bathers. But now the tide has gone out and the people have gone in. Apart from a solitary man walking his dog, I have the whole place to myself.

I was part of that crowd today. I was surrounded by thronging, noisy people, each one seeking a spot in the sun. I don't despise the crowd. At times I love it, and throb with life when I'm part of it. But at other times I need to separate myself from it. That's why I'm down here alone at this late hour. I'm trying to reclaim my soul, to steep myself in peace, and to find my own way again.

It would be hard to find a more suitable place. Here one experiences greatness and grandeur. Everything speaks of permanence and timelessness ... the ceaseless ebb and flow of the tide, the sound of the surf that is never stilled, the infinity of sand grains beneath my feet, the horizon which seems so near yet can never be reached, the immensity of the star-strewn sky above me. There is a little bit of eternity on every seashore.

Yet nowhere does one experience one's own finiteness so acutely. I look at the clear footprints I leave behind me in the soft sand, and realise they won't survive even one tide. Suspended between time and eternity, I am at once humbled and elevated.

'The person who is too busy doing good finds no time to be good.' Rabindranath Tagore

'Wherever we are or wherever we are going, we have our cells with us. For our brother body is the cell, and the soul is the hermit who dwells in it.' Francis of Assisi

'I refresh myself from day to day at the origional source, life itself, and I rest from time to time in prayer.' Etty Hillesum

'In those seasons, of solitude and stillness, I grew like corn in the night.' Henry David Thoreau

The Train Stop

The scenery flashed past the windows of the express train. But for all the passengers saw of that scenery the train might just as well have been windowless. Our story concerns only three of the passengers – three, however, who are typical of the kind of people on the train.

The first is Peter who works for a building society, A very ambitious man, he is determined to be successful in his chosen career. He was recently promoted to regional manager, but he has no intention of resting on his laurels. He is married with a young family.

The second is Jack, a sales representative for a shoe company. A non-stop worker, the company thinks very highly of him and pays him a handsome commission on his sales. However, his wife keeps telling him that he is pushing himself too hard.

The third is Margaret. A very generous person, she is the mother of three children, and works as a nurse in the intensive-care unit of a large hospital. She seems to be permanently on the verge of a breakdown. She would like to slow down, but doesn't know how, so many are the demands and pressures on her.

The three frequently met on the train and talked freely about their lives. They were forever bemoaning the fact that though they had plenty of time for their jobs, they had very little time for themselves and their families, and practically none at all for God and the things of the spirit. Ah, if only they had more time, how different their lives would be! Then one day God appeared to them and said, 'I believe you are looking for more time.'

'Yes, Lord," came the immediate reply.

'Well, you'll be pleased to know that I've decided to give you more time,' said the Lord.

More time? Wonderful!

'When will you give it to us, Lord?' they asked.

'What would you say if I were to give it to you when I think you have most need of it?'

'We'll gladly settle for that,' they replied. With that the Lord smiled on them and disappeared.

A week passed. The three again were on the train which, as we have seen, was hurdling along at breakneck speed. Suddenly the train began to slow down, and to their amazement came to a stop at a small station in the middle of nowhere.

It was the last thing they expected or wanted. Peter had an important board meeting at the other end. Jack had an onward connection to make. And Margaret was urgently needed at the hospital. Jumping to their feet, they demanded to know why train had stopped and how long the stop would be. But no one could tell them.

Peter was furious. As a manager he was well used to sorting things out when they got fouled up. They were rightly fouled up now, yet there wasn't a thing he could do about it. Eventually he calmed down a little. 'Now that I'm stuck here, I might as well make use of the time,' he said. With that he got down his briefcase, took out some papers, and began to work. When the train got going again, still angry, he exclaimed, 'About time!'

Jack too was annoyed at the unscheduled stop. He was one of those people who can't bear to be idle. After only a week of vacation he felt he was rusting away like a discarded engine. Getting off the train, he whiled away the time gossipping with some of the passengers. When the train shook itself into life again, he heaved a huge sigh of relief.

Margaret didn't resent the stop quite as much as the other two. She got off the train and, feeling the need to stretch her legs, went for a walk. The station was set in the middle of a wild but beautiful countryside. After a while she sat down by the side of a path leading through a meadow yellow with buttercups.

Everything was bathed in sunshine. Birdsong issued from every bush and tree. As she sat there a delightful feeling of tranquility stole over her. Then she began to think, 'Life is such a beautiful thing. Yet it is rushing by like the scenery past the windows of the express train, and I'm not living it.' She continued to sit there relaxing and reflecting until she heard the whistle of the train. Reluctantly she made her way back to the station, and boarded the train as it was pulling out.

Once again the train swept them forward towards their destinations. It made up the time lost during the stop, so they were able to keep their appointments after all.

That same night God again appeared to them. 'When are you going to give us that time you promised?' Peter and Jack asked at once.

'I just gave it to you,' God answered calmly. 'I stopped that train especially for you three today. I gave you the most precious time of all time out – or time for yourselves.'

The three were flabbergasted. Turning to Peter and Jack, God said, 'If you wish I can give you more of this time.'

'No thanks,' came the reply from both of them.

Then, turning to Margaret, God asked, 'And how about you? Do you want more time?'

'No thanks, Lord,' she replied. 'During that train stop I learned a great lesson. I learned that I have all the time I need. But there is one thing I would like to ask.'

'And what is that?' said the Lord.

'Please give me the wisdom to use well the time you have given me so liberally.'

And the Lord answered, 'That I will gladly do.'

'It is always in the midst, in the epicentre, of your troubles that you find serenity.' Antoine de Saint Exupery

'In our restless and impoverished lives, every occasion to withdraw, however briefly, from everyday life and to reflect on the world and our selves, is a blessing.' Hermann Hesse

'Merely to reflect on the transience of our lives and undertakings, is a kind of purification and a test as well, even though it may shame us and wound our pride.' Hermann Hesse

'A jar of sunseed oil, shaken until it is cloudy, needs to stand a while for the dregs to settle to the bottom and for the rest to regain its sunny, transparent colour.' Alexander Solzhenitsyn

The Fretful Apple Tree

Though the apple tree is in the prime of life and in the full bloom of health, life is dark, sombre and serious. It's not that its living conditions are bad. The opposite would be nearer the truth.

It looks with incomprehension at the birches which grow nearby. 'What a light-hearted and carefree attitude they have to life,' says the apple tree to itself. 'They produce nothing, not even the humblest berry. They have no pretensions to greatness. Yet they are blessed with a happiness that seems to elude me.'

It turns green with envy when it looks at the surrounding beeches. 'What an enormous amount of timber is contained within their gigantic trunks, timber that one day will be used to make tables, chairs, and maybe whole houses,' says the apple tree again. 'Compared with them I am only a misshapen dwarf. I can't even entertain the hope of being used to make a handle for a broom. And yet,' it added thoughtfully, 'I have one advantage over them. Whereas they produce lots of timber, I produce something far rarer and more precious. I produce delicious apples '

It hates winter. In its view, winter is meant to be endured rather than lived. Winter strips it of its leaves. Of course it strips the beeches too. However, in doing so it serves to draw attention to the magnificence of their arrow-straight trunks. But when it strips the apple tree, it cruelly exposes all those hollows, clefts and knots of which it is secretly ashamed.

It pines for spring. Spring not only bestows a new crop of leaves on it, but decks it out in bright and beautiful blossoms as well. But with those blossoms comes a new crop of anxieties. So many things can go wrong between the apearance of the first blossom and the first ripe apple. And what if the new crop of apples should fail to measure up to the old one? In fact simply to measure up is not good enough. It has to surpass it.

It revels in summer. The days are filled with hazy sunshine and the droning of innumerable bees. By now the blossoms have turned into young apples. Yet it is glad to see the end of summer, because it means the beginning of autumn which of course is harvest time

At harvest time it becomes the centre of attention, especially when the crop is good. Passersby stop to admire the apples, and people come from far and near to get some of them. But, alas, its glory is fleeting. It fades just as soon as the apples are picked. And how rough the pickers can be! They descend on the tree like a pack of wolves, threatening to tear it apart limb from limb. After the apples are gone the tree is left with a hollow feeling. 'It's terrible to be loved not for oneself but only for what one produces,' it says sadly.

Last winter was a particularly long and severe one. The snow lingered on until early May, and the frost dallied even longer. The blossoms were late in appearing. When eventually they did appear, the birds, starved of their usual rations, took an unusually high toll. In summer only a handful of stunted apples appeared on the tree. The harvest was reaped just last week. It was an extremely poor one. The tree was plunged into gloom. 'People forget the good harvests, and remember the bad ones,' it moaned.

I love the little apple tree but I fear for its future. What worries me is this. If it can feel so bad after just one bad harvest, how will it feel when the winter of old age sets in, and there won't be any harvest at all.

The Seed, the Sower and the Soil
Matthew 13:4-9

Parents, teachers, and preachers have one thing in common. They all are sowers. They are forever sowing words in the minds and hearts of those in their care. What a lot of time and energy they expend in doing so. Yet much of what they sow never produces a harvest. Why is this? Perhaps the mistake they make is to place all their hope in words. The greatest and deepest lessons are not taught with words at all.

I once made a retreat in a very beautiful spot in northern Italy. It was still early in the year. The nights were freezing but the days were filled with sunshine. The retreat house stood on an elevation overlooking valleys fringed with pine trees. To the north and west of us was a rim of snow-capped mountains.

It was a ten-day retreat. The retreat master waxed long, earnestly and with no little eloquence, on the Spiritual Exercises of St Ignatius. No doubt what he said impressed me at the time and had some effect on me. Yet today I can't recall a single thing he said. Nevertheless, I have fonder memories of that retreat than of any other. I know exactly why. The surroundings spoke eloquently to me.

In my mind's eye I can still see them. I can see the valleys filling up with darkness each evening like a bright glass filling up with Guinness. I can see the snow-capped peaks glowing like giant torches in the sky at sunrise and sunset.

The whole experience awakened something in me which up to this had been asleep. It planted something in me, the fruits of which still nourish my spirit. It continued to speak to me long after the words of the retreat master had faded into oblivion. Indeed, it continues to speak to me. Even today I'm reaping a harvest from it.

Every moment, and every event in our lives, plants something in our souls. Only time will tell what the harvest will be.

• • •

The seed is the word of God. But what about the veritable blizzard of other words which, thanks especially to television and radio, daily and hourly are falling into the soil of our minds and hearts? How loud and insistent these words are. It's almost impossible to ignore them. How can we hear or even recognise God's quiet word in the midst of this din? We have to create a little bit of stillness and quietness in order to be able to do so.

• • •

Just because a word is sown in the head, doesn't mean that it will automatically put down roots. It may well go in one ear and out the other. Or we may retain it for a while but not long enough for it to bear fruit. It has a much better chance of staying with us and bearing fruit if it is sown in the heart.

In memorising something, we talk about learning it 'off by heart'. This is an interesting expression. Yet it would seem, on reflection, that 'off by head' would be a more accurate one. But maybe 'off by heart' is nearer the mark after all. Because the things that remain in our memory are those that are lodged in the heart.

Just as the seed needs the soil, so the word needs a receptive heart. Unfortunately the heart is not always receptive. The earth responds to the rain and sun so that even the desert blooms. But the arid human heart has the power to resist so that it remains barren.

It's not simply a question of remembering the word, but of doing it. One of the ways of telling a false ruby from a true one is by means of the light. In the case of a false ruby, the light goes straight through the stone. In the case of a true one, the light remains inside it, bringing it to life and setting it on fire.

With some people, the word of God goes in and comes straight back out. They are mere hearers of the word. Only those who 'keep the word' are transformed by it.

The harvest we reap was sown, not just by our own hands, but by innumerable and often unremembered other hands – those of our parents, grandparents, teachers, friends, strangers ... These dear people dropped seeds of advice, instruction, encouragement ... into the soil of our minds and hearts during the springtime of our lives. Without this army of sowers how small our harvest would be. It's no exaggeration to say that all we do is reap what others have sown.

'What rain is to others, the word of God is to us Jews. It nurtures our lives; without it we'd wither like wheat in a drought.' Elie Wiesel

'A void exists between what is said and what is heard.' Elie Wiesel

'Words and silence are not in conflict – they complete and enrich one another.' Elie Wiesel

Weeds among the Wheat
Matthew 13:24-30

A farmer had a field in which the soil was deep and rich. When spring came around he tilled it thoroughly and sowed good seed in it. This done, he sat back in expectation of a bumper harvest.

Soon it looked as if his expectations would be fulfilled. A host of sturdy green shoots sprang up, covering the field from end to end. It brought joy to his heart to see them sway in the wind and dance in the sun. He immediately erected a high fence around the field to protect the crop from predators.

He would go out each morning to feast his eyes on the field. However, one morning when he cast his eyes over it he got a terrible shock. He saw weeds growing among the young shoots of corn. Not just a few weeds here and there, but weeds everywhere.

Now, had it been a piece of waste ground, and the seed of poor quality, he would have understood. But weeds in his best field where he had sown excellent seed! It was the last thing he expected to see. He was desperately disappointed. It hurt like a blow. When he looked at the field now, all he could see were the weeds. The wheat seemed to have disappeared.

'What did I do wrong?' he asked himself. He concluded that some evil power was responsible for the weeds. But wherever they came from, they had no right to be in his good field. They were ruining what promised to be an excellent crop. He would have to get rid of them. But how?

The obvious answer was to pull them up. Though simple in theory, this proved impossible in practice. When he took a close look at the weeds, he found that they were growing so close to the stalks of wheat that he could not uproot them without uprooting the wheat as well. He was sorely tempted to plough up the whole field and start all over again. But it was too late in the season for that. Moreover, who was to say that the same thing wouldn't happen next time round? Besides, to plough the crop up would mean conceding victory to whatever evil power was working against him.

So what did he do? Well, for one thing he calmed down. This enabled him to see things in better perspective. So what if there were some weeds in his precious field! There was wheat there too, wheat that was just as green and vibrant as ever. He would have to be humble and patient. He would have to get up off his easy chair and work harder on the wheat. He would have to coax and encourage it in the hope that it would outgrow the weeds.

So he set to work. It wasn't easy. At times he was on the brink of despair. 'Ah!' he exclaimed, 'were it not for these confounded weeds I could still be sitting back relaxing.' What he found hard to accept was the fact that those weeds would be there right until the day of the harvest.

But he tried to concentrate on the wheat. This proved a great help. When he looked closely at it he noticed that it was by reaching and straining upwards that it grew. He took heart from this because it meant that by making the wheat struggle harder, the weeds were actually having a beneficial effect on the crop. They were making him work harder too, and this he realised was no bad thing either.

When the harvest day arrived he was able at long last to separate the weeds from the wheat. This gave him great satisfaction. But what gave him even greater satisfaction was the fine harvest that resulted.

Even though it fell short of the hundred per cent he had originally been hoping for, the quality was excellent, and it was more than adequate to meet his needs and the needs of his family.

And for some strange reason, he got more satisfaction from reaping this harvest than any other.

A Cruel Blow

Like the farmer, we all enjoy a honeymoon period. But then one morning, sooner or later, we wake up to find weeds growing in our precious field – a friend on whom we were relying lets us down, a child for whom we had high hopes and done so much goes wrong, our marriage partner proves unfaithful ...

It comes not just as a disappointment but also as a very great shock. And hurtful in the extreme – it hits you in the gut. It shatters your faith in the right order of the universe, in humanity, even in God. What made the appearance of the weeds so hurtful to the farmer was the fact that he wasn't expecting them – especially not in that field.

The badness of bad people comes as no great surprise. We expect it, and so are able to forearm ourselves against it. But the badness of good people – that is something else! It takes us by surprise. It catches us with our defences down. The treachery of a friend is much more hurtful and difficult to deal with than the treachery of an enemy.

Writing about Auschwitz, Primo Levi says:

> There is not a prisoner who does not remember his amazement that the first threats, the first insults, the first blows did not come from the SS but from other prisoners, from 'colleagues', from those who wore the same striped tunic that they, the new arrivals, had just put on ... One entered hoping at least for the solidarity of one's companions in misfortune, but the hoped-for allies, except in special cases, were not there ... This brusque revelation, which becomes manifest from the very first hours of imprisonment, was so harsh as to cause the immediate collapse of one's capacity to resist. For many it was lethal. It is difficult to defend oneself against a blow for which one is not prepared. (*The Drowned and the Saved*, pp. 9, 23, 24)

What to Do?

What are we supposed to do about the weeds? To pull them up would seem to be the sensible thing to do. Many opt for this solution. There are people who want a 'clean' Church. If they had their way sinners would be excluded. Only saints would be admitted. Such a Church would be a very small one. In any case, this would be to turn the Gospel upside down. A Church which admitted only saints would make as little sense as a hospital that admitted only healthy people.

There are also those who want a 'clean' society. Naturally they are convinced they themselves would survive the purge. These seem to believe that evil is done only by bad people. They blame all the evils in the world on a limited but inveterate number of evil people. They think that if we got rid of these then we would have a perfect world. What they fail to realise is that evil is done not just by evil people. It is done by the purest and best of people. If evil were done only by evil people, the world would be a far better place.

Even if to pull up the weeds would seem the sensible thing to do, the fact remains that it can't be done without a price – some of the wheat would be lost too. It is a delusion to think that we can split life into halves, and call one half honey, and the other gall; then grasp the honey and leave the gall. If we want to drink deeply from the well of life, we must be prepared to drink the bitter as well as the sweet.

We have to let the weeds be. However, this does not mean we are to give evil a complete free hand. No. Evil must be resisted. It's just that we must find a way of doing so without doing further evil. We must not resist evil with evil. We must resist it with good.

Coexistence

Though the weeds make life a great deal more difficult for us, their presence is not altogether a bad thing. It could even be argued that the weeds have a positive role to play. Contradictory things can and do coexist happily. Opposites are necessary. Fruit grows from the meeting of opposites – male and female.

Which are the trees that grow up straightest and most shapely?

You might think it is those that grow in freedom, those out in the open fields with nothing to hinder them. But it is not so. These trees take their time in growing. As a result, their trunks get gnarled and twisted.

The trees that grow best are those that grow in the forest where they are hard pressed on all sides by competitors bent on robbing them of a share of the sunlight. This makes them drive towards the sun with all the more determination and speed. The result is that their trunks are straight and shapely.

Who are the people who grow best, who turn out to be the best specimens of humanity? One might think it would be those who are surrounded by comforts. But it is not so. Those who grow best are those who have to struggle. Provided they don't go under, struggle brings out the best in people. We grow when challenged. Our very problems can become our salvation.

It has even been claimed, paradoxically, that the existence of evil is a proof of the existence of God – if the world consisted solely and exclusively of goodness, truth, and justice, God would not be necessary, for then the world would be God. Another thing: good and evil must exist so that human beings can make a choice of their own free wills. If we could choose only the good, how would virtue be possible?

The parable, while being realistic, is also very encouraging and hopeful. When the weeds are getting us down, we must hang on, trusting that God will see that they do not deprive us of a harvest. In the end, good will triumph. Truth and goodness are invincible.

'If man did not have to choose between good and evil, life would lose its meaning.' Laurens van der Post

'God exists because evil exists.' Nicolas Berdyayev

'Compassion and brutality can coexist in the same individual and in the same moment, despite all logic.' Primo Levi

'Even in hearts that are overwhelmed by evil, one small bridge-head of good is retained. And in the best of all hearts, there remains an unuprooted small corner of evil.' Alexander Solzhenitsyn

Partners with God

This is what the kingdom of God is like. A man throws seed on the land. Night and day, while he sleeps, when he is awake, the seed is sprouting and growing; how, he does not know. Of its own accord the land produces first the shoot, then the ear, then the full grain in the ear. And when the crop is ready, he loses no time: he starts to reap because the harvest has come. (Mark 4:26-29).

The man did his part – he sowed the seed. Having done that, he could do no more. Things were now out of his control. The one thing he wanted to see happen, namely, for the seed to grow, he couldn't do anything about. All he could do was wait in humility, patience, and hope. But while he was waiting a great power was quietly at work – the power that lies at the heart of all living things.

There is something we can do and have to do. But that done, we have to acknowledge that we can't do everything. In fact, the most important thing of all we cannot do. It can't be imposed from out-side. It must spring from inside. In the great processes of growth, healing, recovery, spiritual progress ... we are only facilitators. Our job is to create the conditions, then another power has to take over.

The parable of the wheat and the weeds shows that there is a power working against us – the power of evil. The present lovely lit-tle parable shows us that there is an almighty power working for us. We can only sow the seed. Then God has to take over. And God does take over. All this is beautifully expressed by Tagore in one of his poems.

On many an idle day have I grieved over lost time. But it is never lost, my Lord. You have taken every moment of my life in your own hands.

Hidden in the heart of things you are nourishing seeds into sprouts, buds into blossoms, and ripening flowers into fruitfulness.

I was tired and sleeping on my idle bed and imagining all work had ceased. In the morning I woke up and found my garden full with wonders of flowers. (*Gitanjali*)

• • •

When God was creating the world, we're told it occurred bit by bit. God made the trees, the grass, the animals, the birds, and so on. As all this was being done, the angels kept asking, 'Is the world finished yet?' To which God would reply with a simple 'No.'

Finally God made people, and said to them, 'I am tired. I want you to finish the world. If you agree to do so, then I promise to be your partner.' They agreed. After this, whenever the angels enquired of God if the world was finished, the reply would come, 'I don't know. You'll have to ask my partners.'

After gathering in a bountiful harvest, the farmer took off his cap. Then standing there in the middle of the empty cornfield, he looked up to heaven and said, 'Thank you, Lord.' And the Lord looked down and said, 'And thank you. *We* did a good job.'

Small Beginnings

The kingdom of heaven is like a mustard seed which a man took and sowed in his field. It is the smallest of all the seeds, but when it has grown it is the biggest shrub of all and becomes a tree so that the birds of the air come and shelter in its branches. (Matthew 13:31-32)

Many, if not all, great undertakings begin in small and often hidden ways. Examples: a building begins with one brick on another, a book begins with one word on a page, a journey with a first step, a forest fire from a single spark, a giant oak from an acorn, a huge river from a tiny spring, a lifelong friendship from a chance encounter.

Seeds need the darkness, isolation, and cover of the earth in order to germinate. Therefore, for something to begin small, hidden, anonymous, is an advantage. It means it can develop away from publicity. There are no pressures. No burden of expectations. It can develop at its own pace. There is no hurry. Hurry ruins so many things.

Hence the importance of beginnings, of taking care of things in their beginnings, of the small in the accomplishment of the great. If you wish the adult to turn out well, then take good care of the child. We ignore the small at our peril. It is not the mega-rows that lead to marriage breakup, but the mini-rows. The treacheries which are destined to reach furthest in their consequences do not begin in an obvious or dramatic way. They begin humbly and unostentatiously, to bear their bitter fruit in maturity. We ascend the heights or sink into the depths a step at a time.

How did Christ begin his great work, the salvation of the world? You might have expected a grand beginning, a great public launching of his campaign, such as politicians go in for. A great mobilisation, or even a mass conscription. Why not? Wasn't the cause so right and so urgent?

Instead, what do we find? He began simply, quietly. No fanfare. No fireworks. No public launching. He began by calling a few people – two in facts (John 1:39). It was as simple as that. He began with personal contact, and that's how his work developed. It was passed on from person to person by word of mouth.

We shouldn't be surprised at this. Things which begin with a splash often peter out. Whereas those which begin quietly put down deep roots, grow steadily, and survive to produce fruit that lasts.

So, if there is something which we want to do, let us not hesitate and think too much. Let us make a start, however small. Let us take one step. Let us plant one seed. Let us trust that if our cause is good, God will support us, and it will grow and prosper.

Einstein's parents were very worried about him because he started to talk comparatively late (at two years) and they consulted a doctor. His Greek teacher said to him, 'You'll never amount to anything.' There was as yet little sign of his future greatness. But his teacher and parents judged him too soon. Some people develop slowly and late, but are all the better for that.

A Remarkable Lady

Lucy is a remarkable lady, though to look at her you would never suspect this. She is not nearly as big or robust as the other gulls. Her vital statistics are easily accounted for. She measures sixteen centimetres from tail to bill, and thirty centimetres from wingtip to wingtip.

Her short webbed feet are nothing to write home about. However, she doesn't use them very much for walking. This way they don't undermine her self-image. Though not lacking in colour, she is no rainbow. Her most peculiar feature is a cute little black skull cap which she wears in all kinds of weather.

Nothing very remarkable so far. Correct. Yet this same little lady is a member of the boldest migratory tribe on earth – the arctic tern. Each year she embarks on a journey which takes her from high within the arctic circle to deep within the antarctic circle, and back again, a round trip of some 22,000 miles. Just think of this: each of those miles has to be beaten out with those two small wings.

Look after the steps and the journey will take care of itself.

'Obscurity is the privilege of young things.' Karen Blixen

'A seed hidden in the heart of an apple is an orchard invisible.' Kahlil Gibran

'*How little stir the real miracles cause! How simple are the most vital events.*' Antoine de Saint Exupery

'*This is the beginning of every decline: to take large matters seriously and neglect small ones.*' Hermann Hesse

'*Deal with the difficult while it is still easy; deal with the big while it is still small.*' Lao Tzu

The Empty House

Jesus told a brief but disturbing little story about an evil spirit which went out of a man and wandered through arid country looking for a suitable place to rest. Unable to find such a place, it decided to return to its original abode. When it came back it found the place swept, tidied, and empty. So the spirit went off, collected seven other spirits, all more evil than itself, and they came back and took possession of that house, so that the last state of the man was worse than the first. (Matthew 12:43-45)

The story is about emptiness. It shows what a dangerous state this can be.

Unfinished Job

Winter was on the retreat. Every day that passed saw its grip on the land become more tenuous. But in its wake it left a corpselike garden. The only signs of life were the weeds, already off to a flying start.

Then one morning the gardener appeared, complete with a brand-new spade. It looked as if, bored with months of enforced idleness, he couldn't wait to get started. He attacked the plots systematically. He dug slowly but steadily. With a firm thrust of the sole of his boot he sank the spade into the soil.

Each time he brought it up, it was loaded with a large cargo of rich dark soil. He turned it upside down and ran the spade through it a couple of times. And so on to the next spadeful. The birds were having a rare feast. They followed him around, gobbling up the slugs before they could worm their way back down to safety.

He was a patient man. Not a square inch of soil escaped his spade. Everthing was upturned. Plot by plot the garden gave way before him. It took him the best part of two weeks to complete the job. But when it was finished it was a joy to behold. The garden had been transformed. There was a fresh look about everything, and a fine earthy smell pervaded the entire place.

I went away and did not get back until July. When I looked in on the garden I got a terrible shock. It was covered with weeds of every description. For reasons unknown to me, the gardener had neglected the most important thing of all – to sow the seed.

• • •

The house of the soul may be spiritually empty. The house of the heart may be empty of love. Both of these states are potentially dangerous. An empty house is an open invitation for unwelcome guests to come and squat, all the more so if the house is clean and tidy. It's not easy for us to admit and confront our essential emptiness. When we do so, we are tempted to try to fill the void with things or activity.

We all suffer from loneliness at one time or another. The thing that makes loneliness unbearable is not lack of human company but inner emptiness. Before God all of us are empty. However, this emptiness can be an opportunity for grace. The ideal container to take to a well is an empty one. The fact that we are empty, and admit it, means that God can fill us from God's own abundance.

'The anguish I experience when I am alone, isolated, and vulnerable is favourable ground for the forces of evil.' Jean Vanier

'In most hearts there is an empty chamber waiting for a guest.' Nathaniel Hawthorne

Tempted by the Good

Temptations try to lure us away from the following of Christ. When we think of temptations, we immediately think of evil things. However, it is not only evil which keeps us from following Christ. Good can do so just as effectively.

It is not just when the path is hard and strewn with obstacles that we fail to reach the goal, but also when it is easy and littered with attractions. In the latter case we are tempted to dally along the way, or to detour. We allow ourselves to be sidetracked, so that before we know it we've forgotten our goal, spent our energy, and wasted our strength. Earthly food dulls the appetite for heavenly food. There are no shortage of examples of this in the Gospels.

It wasn't evil which prevented the rich young man from becoming a disciple of Christ. He had done no evil. What was it then? It was something which is good in itself – wealth.

When Jesus came to the house of Martha and Mary, it wasn't something bad which kept Martha from listening to him. It was something good, even praiseworthy – the details of hospitality.

Those who refused the invitation to the banquet were not acting from bad motives, but from perfectly good ones. One man wanted to go and inspect a piece of land he had bought. Another wanted to go and try out some oxen he had bought. And a third was newly married. However, though their reasons for staying away were perfectly good, the effect was the same as if they had been perfectly vile – they allowed the banquet to pass them by.

The thorns which choked the seed – what were they? 'The worries and cares of this world and the lure of riches.' Again, things not bad in themselves.

Hence, in our efforts to follow Christ, we may have more to fear from the good than from the bad. After all, when we see something which is manifestly evil, it is more likely to repel than to attract us. But when we see something which is manifestly good, we are likely to be attracted by it. Hence it poses more danger.

'Set a bird's wings with gold and it will never fly.' Rabindranath Tagore

'If the desert had been full of beguiling oases instead of snakes, hunger and thirst, the Israelites would never have reached the promised land.' Carlo Carretto

Calling Down Fire

Once Jesus and his disciples approached a village in Samaria, no doubt looking for refreshments and accomodation. However, when the villagers heard that he was heading for Jerusalem, they refused to receive him. The sons of thunder, James and John, took a very dim view of their refusal, and said to Jesus, 'Lord, do you want us to call down fire from heaven to burn them up?' But he rebuked them, and they went off to another village. (Luke 9:51-56)

The reaction of the two disciples not only surprises us but also shocks us. One would have thought that after all the time they had spent with Jesus, they would have known by now that this was not his way of doing things. What they wanted was not just an act of re-taliation, but one of sheer barbarism. Theirs was the kind of thinking that produced the Crusades – those who oppose us are not just our enemies but God's too.

Yet, on reflection, their reaction shouldn't surprise us. In similar circumstances any of us, church-going and God-fearing people, would in all probability have reacted in the same way. All we have to do is look into our hearts to see the truth of this. Are we not con-stantly surprised, shocked, and humbled at the things that arise within us when we are opposed or threatened, even in small ways?

As far as Jesus was concerned, the question of punishment didn't arise. Even had it arisen, you cannot inflict a vast, blanket punishment. It would not only be unjust but outrageous as well.

One day I was a passenger in a friend's car. We were coming into a village when another car, approaching from a side road, pulled right out in front of us. Fortunately my friend is a very alert driver. He spotted the danger at once and jammed on the brakes. Though we got quite a shock we were unharmed. My friend retained his cool. But I lost my rag completely. The offending driver turned out to be a woman. On the far side of the village we started to overtake her. I wanted my friend to let her know what a dreadful thing she had done. If it was me, I'd have flashed the lights, honked the horn, and shaken my fist at her. One way or another I'd have taught her a lesson.

But my friend overtook her as if nothing had happened. When I pointed out to him that I thought he was remiss in not punishing her he replied, 'I refuse to punish the guilty if it means punishing the innocent at the same time.'

For a moment I didn't see his point. But then I looked back and saw that the woman had three young children in the car.

It is infinitely better to allow ten guilty people to go free than to punish one innocent person.

'I hate him not because he is my enemy, or because he hates me, but because he arouses me to hatred.' Elie Wiesel

'We justify the evil we do to our brother because he is no longer a brother, he is merely an adversary.' Thomas Merton

'Punishment if it is collective cannot be just.' Primo Levi

'I do not believe in collective guilt, nor in collective responsibility.' Elie Wiesel

Do Not Resist Evil

'Offer the wicked man no resistance.' (Matthew 5:39)

The Warder

When Tom joined the prison service he was a kind and gentle man. He started out with a very positive attitude towards the prisoners. He knew they were no angels, but he had no prejudices against them. He firmly believed that even the hardest of them could be reformed.

However, there was one thing he really hated. That was bullying. He had been a victim of it himself as a school boy. He soon discovered that bullying was rampant among the prisoners. The weak were mercilessly bullied and preyed upon by the strong.

At first he turned a blind eye to it. But when he could no longer do this, he tried to find excuses for it. However, it gradually got to him. He could see that the more the bullies got away with, the bolder they became. Finally he decided to do something about it.

He tried reasoning with the bullies, but they just laughed at him. Reluctantly he concluded that there was only one course open to him. That was to dish out to the bullies the same kind of treatment they dished out to others. And he was well equipped to do this, for he was tall, strong, and superbly fit. Thus, when he saw some bullying going on, he would take the offender aside and give him a thorough going-over.

This went on for a number of years. At the end of that time the one who had changed most was Tom. He who hated bullies with an undying hate, was now the biggest bully in the prison.

People tend to become what they oppose.

Violence Breeds Violence

Dostoyevsky tells how as a young boy he was being taken by his father away from the city. Being young, he was naturally full of dreams and hopes for the new life which was opening up before him. Soon, however, he got a harsh lesson in reality.

They stopped at an inn for refreshments. While there, a government official came in and quickly downed a few large vodkas. Then he rushed out to his troika and, without a word of explanation, fell on the poor unfortunate driver, a peasant lad, beating him with his fists. Then he ordered him to get going. The driver's response was to bring the whip whistling down the backs of the horses with all his might. Beside themselves with fear and pain, the animals set off at full gallop.

Our pain and hurt can so easily turn into rage, with the result that we take it out on others. Most people are not satisfied until they have unloaded onto their underlings the injury received from above.

Containing Evil

Anyone who has had to deal with a spillage of a substance such as ink or oil knows what a messy business it is. Unless you act quickly it will ruin everything. So what do you do?

You grab the nearest piece of material you can find. Alas, this material may turn out to be hard and resistant. Instead of containing the spillage, it helps to spread it.

But if you find a material which is absorbent you are made. In no time you have contained the spillage. Then slowly and surely you go back and mop up the whole thing. In the end you may be lucky enough to get it all, so that there is no trace of the spillage left.

The material that resists the ink or oil suffers no damage to itself. But the material that absorbs these is practically destroyed by them.

The world has seen, and still sees, many spillages of evil. Practically everybody is revulsed by these. However, instead of helping to contain the evil, some spread it. Fortunately others are willing to absorb some of it, so that it ends with them. Christ is the supreme example of the latter. On the cross he soaked up in his body all the evil of the world.

Those who absorb evil are helping in no less a work than the salvation of the world.

'The only way to overcome evil is to let it run itself to a standstill because it does not find the resistance it is looking for.' Dietrich Bonhoeffer

'He who lives in a pool with crocodiles for long enough, soon grows a snout like one of them.' Zulu saying

'If you don't wish to become a Nazi you must become the opposite.' Elie Wiesel

Words and Deeds

The Budding Artist

The following story comes from a mother.

'My son, John, is very keen on art. And he definitely seems to have a talent for it. His teachers have told him so. His examination results bear this out. Art is the one subject no one has to force him to study.

'But it's early days yet for him. He's still barely an apprentice. He has a very long way to go. To perfect any art requires a lot of hard work, patience, and dedication. I'm not sure that he has what it takes. The one thing he needs right now, however, is encouragement, for art is a lonely business.

'I had often told him how impressed I was with his painting. But somehow this didn't seem to work, or at least it wasn't enough. He didn't seem to believe me. Then it dawned on me that words were not enough. Something else was called for.

'So what did I do? I asked him for one of his favourite pictures. I took this, had it framed, and then hung it in the kitchen. Nothing I ever said to him did as much for his confidence as that simple deed.'

Love needs deeds. Otherwise it is not better than unplanted seed.

The Expert

The rose is one of the most beautiful flowers of all. However, it requires a lot of careful tending if it is to be seen at its best.

In the part of the world I then lived in, we were lucky to have an expert on roses. Damien was his name. His fame had spread far and wide. Proof of this could be seen in the fact that he was in constant demand.

He travelled the length and breadth of the country giving talks and slideshows. He spoke not only with great knowledge of his subject but also with great love of it. Thanks to his talks, many people filled their gardens with exquisite roses.

As I am keenly interested in roses, there was a time when I followed Damien around, lapping up every word that fell from his lips.

One of the very first things I heard him say was, 'No garden can truly be called a garden if it does not possess at least one rose.'

I also heard him say, 'If you wish to have good roses be prepared for a lot of hard work. If you are afraid of thorns then leave roses alone.'

One day I shook hands with him after one of his talks, congratulating him on the excellence of it. As I did so I was conscious of one thing. This was the hand of a master rosegrower.

Naturally I expected his hand to be hard and coarse. Yet to my surprise I found it to be soft and smooth. I looked at it. It didn't bear the slightest mark of a rosethorn.

The following evening I found out why those hands were so well-preserved. I visited the expert in his own home. To my astonishment I found that his garden – that little plot of ground which had been given to him alone to till – was not only bereft of the humblest specimen of rose, but also overgrown with weeds.

'I want to preach the Gospel with my life. Today especially people no longer want to listen to sermons. They want to see the Gospel in action.' Charles de Foucauld

'You have as much learning as you put into practice, and you are as good a preacher as you do what you say.' Francis of Assisi

'Do not say things. What you are stands over you all the while and thunders so that I cannot hear what you say to the contrary.' Ralph Waldo Emerson

'Never recommend anything unless you can provide a little sample of it.' Henry David Thoreau

Asking the Important Questions
Luke 18:18-23

'Master, what have I to do to inherit eternal life?', the young man asked Jesus. This question implies that he had already asked another question, if not of Jesus, then of someone else. That question was: What is the purpose of life? It is obvious that he had got the correct answer to this question. These are the two most important questions in life.

The young ask the important questions, especially the very young. 'Where is Grandpa now that he's dead?' 'Where is heaven?' 'Why did God take away my little sister?' 'Where does God live?' and so on ....

In asking these questions they are usually very direct. They have a habit of going straight to the core of things without any beating around the bush. They often embarrass grown-ups. They also have a tendency to ask these questions at the wrong times – as if there was a wrong time to ask the right question.

Most adults asked these questions when they were young. How come then that so few of them ask them any longer? Here they are, on the train of life, being carried forward inexorably and at an ever increasing speed, but where the train is bound for is no longer a burning issue with them.

Why is this? Could it be that they are so preoccupied with the baggage, or with amusements and distractions, that they simply have no time for such matters? Or could it be that, like the young man who came to Jesus, they have found that it is dangerous to ask such questions? It is not so much the answers they are afraid of, as the consequences of those answers, should they take them seriously.

The young man was a good man. However, it is a lot easier to be good when you are secure. He still had dreams. His riches hadn't yet hardened his heart. He was still asking questions, still searching. This is why he came to Jesus.

Jesus looked at him with love and admiration. He saw that here was a young man who could go a long way if only he could launch him. He didn't beat around the bush with him. He threw down the gauntlet to him, saying, 'Sell all that you own and distribute the money to the poor, and you will have treasure in heaven; then come, follow me.'

The young man stood on the brink of a new world, a challenging and exciting world. However, he realised at once that he could not enter this new world without saying goodbye to his old world. He hesitated. He thought about it. He looked back at that old world and began to weigh up the things he was leaving. Suddenly he realised he couldn't do it. There was too much in that old world which he loved and wanted. So he refused the invitation of Jesus.

Some people are unwilling to let go of a single value in order to acquire a new one. If we fear to lose the pleasures of the old world, we will never taste the joys of the new.

'You are no better for merely desiring things, without striving towards them.' Antoine de Saint Exupery

'People settle down, each in his pothole, calling stagnation happiness.' Antoine de Saint Exupery

Expensive Imitations

An historic auction was about to take place. On sale was a 39-by-30 inch canvas. It contained Van Gogh's famous painting of fifteen sunflowers.

Matthew made sure to get there early. This was an occasion not to be missed. He was going to bid but didn't hold out any real hope of obtaining the painting. But it would be nice to be there nonetheless. He decided to take along his six-year-old son, Brian, for the experience.

The room was crowded long before the auction began. While he waited Matthew never took his eyes off the famous painting. The more he saw of it, the more his heart pined for it. What he wouldn't give to possess it! He felt the tension mount as the moment approached for the painting to come under the auctioneer's hammer. At long last the great moment arrived and the bidding started.

Matthew didn't move in at once. He waited his moment, then went in with his bid. Alas, it was swept away like a drop in a torrent, and he found himself a mere spectator. When Van Gogh finished the painting in 1890 he believed it was worth about 500 francs. Yet at the auction it took less than five minutes for the price to reach £5 million. but it didn't stop there. Eventually it became a straight contest between two anonymous buyers who weren't even there, but were bidding by telephone. There were gasps of astonishment as the price went up in leaps of half a million. Finally it was sold for £24.75 million.

When it was all over Matthew's heart continued to throb from the excitement of it. Though he had told himself from the outset that he had no real chance of obtaining the painting, he still felt a pang of disappointment as he left the room. Before going outside he cast a last lingering glance at the painting.

It was only when he was outside that he realised his son was not with him. In his excitement he had forgotten all about him. He dashed back inside to look for him. Not finding him there he went out again and started to look for him in the grounds. The grounds were filled with all sorts of beautiful flowers. On his way in he had been so preoccupied with the auction that he hadn't even noticed them.

To his great relief, he spotted his son among the flowers. As he drew near him he found that he was examining a host of sunflowers. He was feeling them and smelling them one by one. Though Matthew was upset, he decided not to scold his son. The occasion was too big for that. Instead, as he led him to the car, he began to tell him in as simple a way as he could all about the auction and the incredible price the sunflowers had fetched. But he could see that his son did not share his enthusiasm. When he paused, the questions began to pour out of Brian.

'What do Van Gogh's sunflowers smell like?' he asked.

'They have no smell, son.'

'What do they feel like?'

'No one is allowed touch them. They are kept behind glass.'

'How tall are they?'

'A foot or so.'

'Do they tremble when the wind blows them?'

'Of course not.'

'Do they open up when the sun shines on them?'

'Don't be ridiculous,' said the father, becoming impatient with all the questions.

There was a long pause. Then the son said, 'Daddy, I still prefer my sunflowers.'

Matthew suddenly realised something, and instantly his disappointment vanished. He would never possess Van Gogh's sunflowers. Even if he won the lottery he would not be able to afford them.

'So what!' he exclaimed, thinking aloud. 'I can still have sunflowers. Not expensive imitations but real ones. I can have them any day I wish, and have them for nothing.'

Then turning to his son he said, 'Son, Van Gogh painted those sunflowers so wonderfully because, like you, he first of all found time to admire and love real ones.'

Father and Sons

Luke 15:11-32

In writing a story there comes a moment of great decision: how to end it. Whether to opt for an expected ending or an unexpected one, a happy one or a sad one? Of course one could always leave it open.

When Jesus composed what is surely his greatest story, he too was faced with these options. I'm glad he didn't leave it open. I'm glad he opted for the ending he did – an outrageously unexpected and happy one.

Still, there are those who believe that he went overboard. These feel that it is a very unfair and unjust story. Indeed, that it gives a licence to sin. They feel sorry for the older son. They believe the younger son got away with murder. He should have been punished. He should have been taught a lesson.

Those who feel like this obviously identify completely with the older son. They see themselves as the faithful one. But does this not smack of self-righteousness? Which of us can say that we have always been faithful? Do we not all squander God's grace and misuse God's gifts? Do we not all need to return? Therefore, which of us would like to be treated by God according to strict justice? Do we not all need more mercy than justice?

Those who say that the younger son should have been punished show how superficially they have read the story. Their attitude betrays a shallow understanding of human nature and of life. Let us look at the story again, to see if we can enter more deeply into it. Let us begin by following the footsteps of the younger son.

The Younger Son

'Give me my share of the property,' said the younger son.

He was going to have his fling. He didn't care what others thought or who might get hurt. He was going to break out, to shake off all obligations, duties, loyalties, ties and restraints. And shake them off he did. He set off for a foreign country where he wouldn't be known and so could live as he wanted. He couldn't get there fast enough. He was borne along on the wings of the wind.

Once there he began to live it up. He had everything money could buy. He gave no thought for tomorrow. With reckless abandon he gave free rein to all his instincts. He discovered life from the worst side – a cheap, distorted version of it. He knew well that he was being irresponsible, but he deluded himself that he was living this kind of life temporarily. He tried to convince himself that he was happy, but this was not true. He had a surfeit of pleasure but no joy.

Still, he went on down this same road, and would have continued to do so but for one thing – the well of money ran dry. Suddenly the bright lights faded, all doors were closed against him, and he found himself walking the streets in the rain.

Pretty soon he started to feel sorry for himself. 'Nobody cares about me,' he said to himself. 'There is no one to help or pity me. Yet once I was home, happy and loved.' The thought of home sent a pang of remorse through him. For the first time he realised what he had done to his father and felt bad about it. He couldn't believe, couldn't conceive, how he had acted as he did. If he had been ill-treated it would not have been so bad. But he was loved. There was no justification for it.

Though he saw how grievously he had wronged his father, he was as yet unable to take the decisive action that was required to put matters right. Instead of going home to atone for his wrong, he took a job minding pigs – he was that desperate for something to eat. This quickly brought him to his senses.

One night he said to himself, 'It is far more honourable to admit one's mistakes than to let matters go on to the irrevocable. I will go back to my father and tell him I'm sorry.'

'I will go back.' Brave words! But would he be able to carry them out when the sun rose the next day? Would he have the courage to face back home as he was? He was coming back laden not with honour and glory but with shame and disgrace. He wasn't coming back as a conquerer, eager to lay his laurels at his father's feet. He was coming back as a renegade.

What a wretched experience it had turned out to be! Instead of a dream come true, it had turned into a nightmare. Others would never be able to understand the suffering and pain he had been through. They would think that he had a great time. If only they knew the bitterness of betrayal, the loneliness of sin. He had eaten his fill of forbidden fruit and, far from satisfying him, it had left him with a foul taste in his mouth.

It would be hard to describe the pain of that journey back. Every inch was like a mile. His feet were like lead. His heart was trembling. He didn't know what kind of reception he would get. He was taking a terrible gamble. Suppose his father should disown him, as he had every right to do? What would he do then? Everything was out of his hands.

Suddenly he came over the brow of a hill. There it was – the old house. The sight filled him with a mixture of joy and dread. Should he go in by the front door or the back door? Before he could make up his mind he saw a figure running towards him. He stopped. It was his father! Next minute he was in his arms. Words were redundant.

His father had made it so easy for him. He hadn't stood on his dignity and waited for him to come and grovel at his feet. He had come to meet him. He had thrown up a bridge and met him halfway across. He hadn't just accepted him back. He had welcomed him back. Suddenly he realised the depth of his father's love for him, and his heart overflowed with love for his father. Before one can know what love is, one must have a fall and pick oneself up again.

Do we still think that the younger son ought to have been punished and taught a lesson? The truth is he had already been punished – punished severely – by life. He had suffered more than enough – desertion by friends, loneliness, homesickness, desperation, humiliation, hunger … On top of all these, there was the sense of betrayal that haunted him. The last thing he needed was more punishment. In any case, what would punishment have achieved? You can't punish people into being better.

Nor did he need to be taught a lesson. He had already learned a lesson – something which is far more important. He had learned a bitter lesson, one he was unlikely ever to forget.

Moreover, he did a mighty deed – he had come back home. It's easy to come back when you're successful, or a hero laden with glory. But to come back laden with disgrace: try that and see if it is easy. To knock at the door and have to wait for it to be opened to you. Things are totally out of your control. You don't know whether you will be accepted back or told to get lost.

To understand all this we have to put ourselves into the skin of the younger son, or we must have been through some similar experience ourselves.

'To sin is to suffer.' Jean Paul Sartre

The Older Son

Let us now turn to the older son. Many feel sorry for him, convinced he got a raw deal. They put themselves in his shoes, and so feel they can not only understand his reaction but also endorse it. But we must take a deeper look at him.

All those years the younger son had been away, the older son had been at home, close to his father and doing what was asked of him. However, near and all as he was to his father, he failed to grasp the essential quality of his father, namely, his deep and unconditional love for his children. No doubt he felt that he loved his father. But his was a burdensome love. In truth, what he had was respect rather than love. Respect was invented to fill the empty place where love should be.

Meanwhile his heart was burning with resentment towards his younger brother. His brother was out there somewhere, having a good time – girls, booze, the lot – while he was at home with sweaty face and blistered hands. And his father, instead of forgetting his hobo son, spent his time looking out the front window in the hope that the selfish, ungrateful scoundrel might come back. He ended up hating his brother, and sometimes hating his father for loving him.

Instead of deepening his relationship with his father, what he had been doing was measuring himself against his brother. He felt good because his brother was bad. It was like a moral see-saw: he was on one end of it and his brother on the other end. The fact that his brother was down meant that he was lifted up.

Now, however, his brother had suddenly been lifted up. Naturally he felt he had been let down. Thus, his brother's repentance, instead of being a cause of joy, became a threat to him. The same act that had reconstructed the world of the younger son, shattered the world of the older son.

According to the latter's way of thinking, love was something you had to earn. You had to prove yourself worthy of it. The younger son had proved himself worthy, not of love, but of punishment. Yet he was being loved, madly loved. Whereas the older son, who had been obedient and hard-working, thereby earning his father's love, was pushed into the background and forgotten.

Not surprisingly the older son rebelled. It was so unfair, so unjust! Everything that had been a comfort to him, and which had made his labours and sufferings tolerable and meaningful, was swept away. What good was there in toiling and striving if there were no rewards or punishments?

While we can have some sympathy for him, nevertheless, he cuts a rather sad figure. While in some respects he is a model son, in others he is woefully lacking. Living in a climate of love, we would have expected him to have grown into a young man capable of tolerance, understanding, and compassion. Instead what do we find? We find a young man who is narrow-minded, hard-hearted, and embittered.

We have indeed reason to feel sorry for him. Not because he was unfairly treated by his father – which he wasn't. But because he excluded himself from the banquet which was given to celebrate the fact that his lost brother had been found, his dead brother had come back to life.

Still, in spite of all that has been said, his negative reaction teaches us a valuable lesson. We tend to make a big splash for the one who is away and who comes back home, if only for a brief visit, while we take for granted the one who is at home all the time.

Making a Fresh Start

It is possible to be too obedient as a child, too anxious to please and win approval. We learn to show outwardly what is not inside. When we are too obedient, quiet in church, hard-working at school, and so on, it may be that some unknown rebellion brews inside us which is bound to erupt later on.

Hence, the younger son's act of rebellion may have been necessary in order to achieve a more meaningful obedience. His separation from home and father may have been necessary in order to achieve a greater reunion and oneness of life with his father.

However, this is not to excuse what he did. The story must not be pushed too far. It does not say that it doesn't matter how we live, or what we do, because God is waiting with open arms to forgive us. It does not say it is okay to sin. What it does say is that if, through human weakness or wickedness, we do sin, then we will bring nothing but misery on ourselves. But it also says that we can come back. Our past can be overcome. We can make a fresh start. This is the great lesson of the parable.

One last point. Did everything come right for the younger son now that he had come back? I very much doubt it. It's unlikely that he was able to set aside his old way of life just like that. No doubt some of the mud of sin still stuck to him. He had awakened certain base desires and given free rein to them. They would not go back to sleep overnight.

The Prodigal Mother

The fruit bowl, made of Waterford crystal, had stood on the sideboard for twelve years. Apart from its monetary value it had tremendous sentimental value for its owner, Mrs Murphy. It was a wedding present from her parents, both now deceased. Of course it was never used. Her two children, John (aged ten) and Mary (aged eight), knew how much she valued the bowl, so they kept their distance from it.

But kids being kids this could hardly be expected to go on forever. And it didn't. One rainy day John and Mary had spent the entire morning cooped up indoors. In the afternoon the mother went out for what was to have been a brief trip to the shops. But fate intervened. The car ran out of petrol with the result that she was out of the house for two hours.

Now two hours is a long time in the life of a kid. It proved too long for a busybody such as John to be without supervision. At a certain point he lost his reason and took the bowl down from the sideboard. He was amazed at how heavy it was. Mary kept telling him to put it back, but this only made him all the more daring.

Then he discovered that it was exciting to hold it up to the light and to look through it. It became a myriad of little prisms, each one with a rainbow trapped inside it. Next he got the idea that it would be fun to look at the fire through it. By now he was getting a little casual in the way he handled it.

As he approached the fire he wasn't looking where he was going. He was already trying to look at the fire through the bowl. Now on the floor in front of the fire some toy motor cars were scattered. He stepped on one of these. Suddenly his feet were taken from under him. With that the bowl left his hand and was transformed into a flying saucer. It fell to earth on the stone tiles in front of the fire where it exploded into little pieces.

'Oh, you've broken the bowl! Mother will kill you when she gets home,' Mary cried.

The catastrophe happened during the first hour. The next hour was the worst time of his young life. He went down on his hands and knees and gathered up the pieces. He made a futile effort to put the bowl back together again. Ah, if only he had a magic wand! But, alas! magic wands exist only in fairy stories.

What was he to do? To hide the evidence was out of the question. Well then, maybe he could hide himself, out in the woods or somewhere? He opened the back door, but was driven back inside by a squall of sleety rain. There was nothing for it, therefore, but to face the music.

The wait began. The longer it went on, the worse it got. It was terrible to feel that he had done something which could never be undone. And Mary was not one bit of help to him. He looked again and again at the pieces of what was once a beautiful bowl. How fragile it was. And the thought occurred to him: if such things are so valuable, then why in heaven's name don't they make them unbreakable?

Then he began to reflect on his own condition. He had always thought that he was a rocklike character, unlike his sister who was so brittle that she cried if you as much as pinched her. Now he realised that he was very brittle himself. If someone were to strike him, or to let him fall now, he would break into a million pieces.

At long last the sound of the car was heard in the driveway. 'She's back,' Mary announced as she peeped out through the curtains. John waited in the hallway, the pieces of glass gathered into a shoebox which he held in his hands. Tears were running down his face. He heard his mother insert the key in the lock. Then the door sprang open and she was standing in front of him. He tried to say his rehearsed piece: 'Mother, I broke the bowl. I'm sorry. It was all my fault.' But the words refused to come out.

By now, however, his mother had seen his tears. Letting down her shopping bags, she went over to him. Just as he thought the blows were about to come raining down on his head, he felt her arms encircle him, and heard her say, 'Son, don't worry about the bowl. You are far more important to me than any bowl.'

They were the sweetest words he had ever heard, and he would remember them to his dying day. They transported him from the jaws of hell straight to the gate of heaven. He felt himself being knit together. In the twinkling of an eye he was whole and sound once more. So magic wands did exist in the real world after all!

For the rest of the evening he went around as if walking on air, and couldn't do enough for his mother. Meanwhile Mary went around with a sour look on her face. She was disappointed that her brother hadn't got the trashing she felt he so richly deserved.

Showing Compassion

Counsellors and therapists are told that in dealing with their clients they must at all times control their emotions. They must stay detached. They must maintain a certain aloofness. This advice makes sense. Otherwise they would not be able to maintain the necessary perspective. They would leave themselves open to manipulation and possible take-over by their clients. They would also be in danger of burn-out. Hence, no matter how heart-rending the client's story may be, they must keep their professional cool.

Yet this coolness, this detachment, can be carried too far. The quality of the relationship between therapist and client is of the utmost importance. The attitude of the therapist is far more important than any procedures and techniques. A cold, detached, unsympathetic attitude on the part of the therapist is not conducive to healing.

The patient must experience warmth, sympathy, and care for healing, change, and growth to take place.

Therapy works best when the therapist is affected by the plight of the patient, and is not afraid to let the patient see this. When as a patient you meet someone who seems to understand what it is like to be you, without wanting to analyse you or judge you, then you can blossom and grow in that kind of climate. When you discover that your pain is felt by the person in whom you have confided, it makes you want to get well.

The experts and professionals tend to keep their distance while the amateurs tend to get more involved with their patients. The former often look down on the latter, yet the latter sometimes achieve more. This is not so surprising when you realise that the word 'amateur' comes from the Latin word *amare* which means 'to love'. In the long run, love is the thing that heals.

Jesus was no detached healer. He showed care and compassion for those who suffered. And he wasn't afraid to let the sufferers know that he cared about them. He entered into their pain and shared it before relieving it.

There are many examples of this in the Gospel. '*Feeling sorry. for him* [the leper], Jesus stretched out his hand and touched him.' (Mark 1:41). 'On stepping ashore, he saw a large crowd; and *he took pity on them* because they were like sheep without a shepherd.' (Mark 6:34). On the way to the tomb of Lazarus he actually wept. On seeing this the Jews said, 'See how much he loved him!' (John 11:36).

Medicine for a Wounded Heart

Mark, severely physically handicapped and apparently unable to speak, was locked into a lonely, silent world. The door wasn't actually locked. He was free to leave if he so wished. But apparently he had no wish to do so. He had retreated from the world, if indeed he ever belonged to it. He had cut himself off from life and from other people. So there he remained, joyless and forlorn.

Why had he done this? Because he felt useless and hopeless. He had nothing to live for. No goal, no aim, no purpose. His self-worth was nil. It is sad and tragic when a human being is locked up in himself and unable to communicate. What makes it so sad is the fact that it results in the death of the heart.

From time to time the professionals had made attempts to reach him. But instead of offering him the one thing he desperately needed, and was secretly crying for, namely, intimacy and human warmth, they offered him words. But words proved ineffective, because wounds like his can't be cured by words alone.

Yet a few years later Mark had become an expert ham radio operator. He had so come out of his shell that he was in touch with other radio operators from over thirty countries scattered around the world.

How was the miracle achieved? One day a woman went to see him. Entering his dark, lonely world she said simply, 'Hello, Mark! I'm Claire.' Then she sat down beside him. She did not go away. Now at long last he had a friend, someone who believed in him and cared about him. A spark was lit in his dim life. Gradually this spark turned into a bright gleam. Eventually he followed the gleam. It led him out of his prison.

Love is the only medicine that will heal a wounded heart.

'I have learned that only the physician who feels himself deeply affected by his patients could heal.' Carl Jung

'Loving-kindness, human sympathy, are often more important to the patient than any medicine.' Fyodor Dostoyevsky

'It is an extraordinary thing for a person with a handicap to discover that he is loved.' Jean Vanier

Men at Prayer
Luke 18:9-14

The prayer of the Pharisee went like this: 'I thank you, God, that I am not grasping, unjust, adulterous like the rest of mankind, and particularly that I am not like this tax collector here. I fast twice a week; I pay tithes on all I get.'

The prayer of the tax collector might well have gone like this: 'Lord, look at the Pharisee standing up so that everybody can see him praying. He thinks he's better than everybody else. He despises people like me. See the long robes he's wearing so as to make himself feel holy and attract attention to himself. Everything he does is done, not to bring honour to you, but to win the esteem of others and thus bring honour to himself. He makes sure to get the seats of honour at banquets and in the synagogue. He loves it when people salute him in the marketplace and call him "Rabbi".

'He gets all hot and bothered about silly little rules of his own making, while neglecting the things that really matter – the practice of justice and mercy. He's good at laying down the law for others. He ought to practise what he preaches. He lives off the contributions of widows.

'Ah, Lord, don't be taken in by him. It's all an act, it's all a show. He's not genuine. He may look clean on the outside, like a whitewashed tomb, but inside he's full of corruption. He's the biggest hypocrite on two feet.'

All this and more the tax collector could have said. And the Lord might have added, 'I agree with every word you've said,' because the Lord himself said all these things about the Pharisees. But the tax collector said nothing of the sort. Instead, he simply said, 'God, be merciful to me, a sinner.'

What the Pharisee did was confess the sins of others, while at the same time parading his own good deeds. The tax collector did the exact opposite. He confessed his own sins, and left the sins of others between them and God. As a result the tax collector went home at rights with God, whereas the Pharisee did not. We have Jesus' word for this.

It's easy to get into the habit of confessing the sins of others. But it's dangerous because it prevents us from looking at our own sins. Besides, it's impossible to weigh the sins of others without putting your own finger on the scales.

The successful are always tempted to regard their success as a sort of blessing from God or a reward for righteousness. This leads to judgements being made about the unsuccessful, which are both uncharitable and untrue.

St Francis of Assisi once declared, 'I think that I am the greatest sinner in the world. Yes, without doubt, that is how I see myself.' When someone asked, 'How can you say that? What about all the thieves, fornicators, and murderers in the world?' Francis replied, 'There is no man or woman in the world who would not be more pleasing to God than I am, if God had bestowed on them the graces he has given me.'

'True humility impels you, not to demean yourself, but to open your heart.' Antoine de Saint Exupery

Service Station for Sinners

It's Saturday evening and Fr Murphy is hearing confessions.

A woman comes in and, with tears in her eyes, confesses to having committed adultery. He marvels at the courage and honesty required to make such a clean confession. What joy it gives him to be able to say to her, 'Your sin is forgiven, go in peace.'

A wealthy man comes in and confesses to having been unjust in his business dealings. He is now sorry and wants to make restitution. Fr Murphy is delighted to be able to say to him, 'This day salvation has come to your house.'

A youth comes in and tells how he ran away from home, thus

causing great pain to his parents. Now he regrets what he did and wants to return home. 'There will be joy in heaven tonight because of your decision to be reconciled with your family,' says Fr Murphy.

Next a man comes in and announces, 'It's a year since my last confession.' Fr Murphy thinks to himself, 'A whole year! There will be a nice little harvest of sins to reap.' But then the man proclaims confidently, 'I'm a married man with a family. I go to Mass regularly. I say prayers every day. I'm not conscious of having done anybody any wrong.'

Fr Murphy is taken aback. Perhaps he is dealing with a saint? But he doubts it, because of all people, the saints were the ones who were most convinced of their sinfulness. So he asks himself, 'Does this man realise where he is? This is not a bank where one makes deposits. This is a service station for sinners.'

Should he probe a little? Should he ask the man how he treats his wife? What kind of father he is to his children? How he gets on with his neighbours? But has he not answered these questions already? He does nobody any wrong.

It suddenly occurs to Fr Murphy that the priest and the levite, who passed by the man lying wounded at the side of the road, could have said the same thing. So too could the rich man who left a poor man die of hunger outside his very gate.

What he really should ask him is, 'Do you do anybody any good?' Even though this occurs to him, something prevents him from doing so. He's at a loss to know what he should do for him. However, of one thing he is sure. He cannot announce the Good News to him.

Raindrops Kept Falling on His Head

Once there was a little deer by the name of Raindrops who was born with a defect in one of his front legs. As a result of this he was lame. At first he made light of his affliction. He thought it would go away as he grew up. But it did not go away.

When he realised that his disability was there to stay, he grew resentful, and went into a severe depression. His companions didn't make things easy for him. In an unthinking yet cruel way they mocked him and laughed at his efforts at running.

It pained him to watch those same companions emancipate themselves from their parents, and go off into the great plains in search of adventure. He envied the speed with which they bounded away, the great distances they travelled, and the wonderful stories they had to tell on their return. What he wouldn't have given to be able to join them!

In the early days he did his utmost to do so. But no matter how hard he tried, he didn't succeed. He kept falling on his head. After many bitter failures he finally had to accept defeat. He just could not keep up with the others. He discovered that if he went more than half a mile or so from the stream near which he was born, and which was home for the herd, he could not be sure of making it back.

One good thing, however, resulted from his handicap. He had lots of time to think. Thus he matured quickly and well. He realised that he was not the only deer with a problem. He saw that every deer had troubles of one kind or another. It was just that most of those troubles were not as visible as his was. So he eventually came to accept his limitations, though love them he never would. Even though he continued to suffer the odd bout of loneliness and self-pity, he came to realise that life was not so bad. There were still lots of things he could do, lots of things he could enjoy.

There was something else which helped him come to terms with his handicap. Now and again a tragedy would happen to the herd. It would go too far out into the dry plains. There some of the younger and weaker deer would get separated from the main herd, never to be seen again. At other times a severe drought would occur, and some of the deer would die of thirst before they could get back to the stream.

Now Raindrops was a kind-hearted and compassionate little fellow. It goes without saying, therefore, that these tragedies brought no joy to him. In fact, quite the opposite. Each of those tragedies caused him deep grief. Nevertheless, in a strange way, they had the effect of making him grateful for his disability. It kept him close to the stream. There he had an unfailing supply of green grass to eat and fresh water to drink.

It's the Heart that Matters

It's amazing how often the word 'heart' occurs in the Gospel. Here are some examples taken from Saint Matthew.

'Happy the pure in heart: they shall see God.' (5:8)

'Where your treasure is, there will your heart be also.' (6:21)

'Set your hearts on the kingdom of God first, and on his righteousness, and all these other things will be given you as well.' (6:34)

'Learn from me, for I am gentle and humble in heart, and you will find rest for your souls.' (11:29)

'A man's words flow out of what fills his heart.' (12:34)

'This people honours me only with lip-service, while their hearts are far from me.' (15:8)

'The things that make a person unclean are not the things that go into him, but the things that come out of him, that come out of his heart.' (15:17-18)

'You must forgive your brother from your heart.' (18:35)

This shows the importance Jesus placed on the heart. In the western world we pay far more attention to the head than to the heart. This is especially true in education. We feed the head and starve the heart. In the eastern world, on the other hand, they attach more importance to the heart.

• • •

It is only with the heart that we can see rightly. To see with the eyes only is to be no better than a camera.

It is only with the heart that we can hear rightly. The cry of a needy person may reach our ears, but unless it reaches our heart we will not feel the person's pain, and it is unlikely that we will respond.

It is only with the heart that we can speak rightly. For our words to ring true, they must be spoken from the heart. If they come only from the lips, they will have a hollow sound and will have little effect. They will be like a wind that ripples the surface of the water but leaves the depths untouched.

It is only with the heart that we can give rightly. If our gift does not come from the heart, it doesn't ennoble us or enrich the receiver. It is possible to give generously with the hand and still be a miser at heart.

It is only with the heart that we can work rightly. If our heart is in our work, the work becomes a joy and we put our best into it. But if our heart is not in our work, we are working under the severest handicap of all.

It is only with the heart that we can welcome a person rightly. We may open the door of our home to someone, but unless we make room for him in our heart, he will still be a stranger to us.

It is only with the heart that we can forgive rightly. If forgiveness does not come from our heart, it will not bring us peace, nor will it result in a true reconciliation with the other party.

It is only with the heart that we can repent rightly. If our repentance does not reach our heart, it will not lead to a change of life. It will be like decapitating weeds while leaving their roots intact.

It is only with the heart that we can worship God rightly. If our heart is not in our worship, we are no better than answering machines: our voice is present but we are absent.

• • •

Behind the eyes of each one of us lies a whole world. It is the world of the heart. Much of this world is hidden from us, but we are not totally in the dark. The state of a person's heart can be glimpsed in the face, especially in the eyes. Corruption of heart coarsens the face and darkens the eyes, whereas purity of heart softens the face and causes the eyes to shine.

How can one describe or sum up the heart? Darkness of heart is the blackest night of all. Emptiness of heart is the greatest poverty of all. A heavy heart is the most wearisome burden of all. A broken heart is the most painful wound of all.

When all is said and done it is the heart that matters. To close one's heart is to begin to die. To open one's heart is to begin to live. The world is God's temple. The human heart is God's sanctuary.

Sheep, Shepherds and Wolves

Amos and Abel

Amos and Abel cast their eyes over the assembled sheep. Abel's glance is hurried and superficial. All he sees is a sea of faces. He knows almost nothing of the individual biographies of the sheep. As he was bringing them in, he couldn't fail to notice that some of them were limping, others were thin, and others were constantly itching themselves. But now he can't remember which ones, and is too lazy to find out. Yet these are only the external wounds of the sheep. As for their internal wounds, he doesn't even know they exist.

Amos, on the other hand, is not content to cast a mere glance at the sheep. He looks at them long and searchingly. Nothing escapes his experienced and caring eye. He doesn't see a flock but a collection of individual sheep. Behind each face is a story which is thoroughly familiar to him. His eyes now search for the wounded ones. He spots a lame one. Tomorrow morning he will examine her foot to find out what the problem is. He sees a thin one. Tomorrow he will give him a dose to counter the worms.

But he doesn't limit himself to the external wounds of the sheep. He lovingly searches their faces to discover those that are hurting inside. He sees the anxious face of one whose lamb is overdue. He scrutinises the sad face of one whose lamb was still-born. He dwells on the lonely face of one whose companion died recently. He feels their pain, and resolves to be extra gentle with them.

How do you account for the difference between the two shepherds? Let us take Abel first. For him, caring for the sheep is just a job. He is a hireling. His heart is not in his work. His real life is somewhere else, and his work is interfering with it. He applies himself to shepherding with a mixture of apathy and indolence. Because his self-esteem is not involved in it, he takes no pride in it. He is not a happy person.

Now let us take Amos. For him, caring for the sheep is no mere job. It is more like a vocation. His heart is in it. They are his sheep. Even though you may hear him complain about the hardships of his calling from time to time, he is a happy man. He has found a work which gives meaning and inspiration to his life. In doing it well he becomes a better man.

Becoming a Shepherd

The night was bitterly cold. A slight mist had started to fall. Amos drew the coat more tightly around him. He was a shepherd. Tonight his mind went back to when it all began.

Right from his youth he had dreamed about becoming a shepherd. He wanted nothing else. He loved sheep and wanted to devote his life to them. But in those far-off days he was very naive. His youthful mind was brimming with romantic ideas. To him a shepherd was someone who loved sheep and who devoted himself totally to them. What could be simpler? But now his eyes were being opened. The task of shepherding was turning out to be a far more complicated thing than he had imagined.

How many jobs this one job embraced! At times he was more like a builder than a shepherd, so much time did he spend building and repairing walls and fences. At other times the job required of him the ability of a weather-forecaster. Again at other times it demanded the expertise of a veterinary surgeon, and the skill of a professional tracker. And tonight he was a watchman, no different from countless other watchmen lost in the silence of the night.

'How different the reality is from the dream,' he said to himself. But then another voice said, 'You are now being given the chance to become in earnest what you naively dreamed about when you started out. There is no such thing as a born shepherd. One becomes a shepherd.'

Lost Sheep Looking for the Shepherd

When Paul first left the flock he didn't think of himself as lost. No, he was not lost. He had merely thrown off the constraints of belonging to a flock and being at the beck and call of the shepherd. In other words, he was free.

But that was a good many years ago. It didn't take him long to realise that he was not free but lost. However, even when he realised this, it didn't bother him. He would be found again. But the years went by, years in which by some miracle he managed to elude the claws of the wolf, and he still wasn't found.

Meanwhile, the desire to be part of the flock again was growing inside him. Wouldn't it be lovely, he thought, if one day the shepherd were to come over the hill and say, 'Ah, there you are! I've been looking all over for you. Am I glad I found you. How are you, anyway?' However, he gradually came to accept that this was a forlorn hope.

One day he said to himself, 'I know exactly how the shepherd is thinking. He knows he has lost some sheep from his flock. But he has come to accept that a certain "wastage" is inevitable in these days of unbridled freedom. Therefore, he doesn't hold himself in any way responsible, and so feels no guilt. Besides, he still has a large number of sheep to attend to. These need him and deserve him. He's run off his feet. But he's not complaining. In fact he's quite pleased with himself and feels very fulfilled.'

Then another thing dawned on him. The shepherd was a member of a respected class. He had his good name and reputation to preserve. How could such a man be expected to come to the kind of places lost sheep frequent, or mix with the kind of company they keep? He couldn't do it. It wouldn't be right. He would scandalise the faithful members of his flock.

Thus it gradually came home to him that the shepherd was not looking for him. Worse still, he wasn't even thinking about him. He had forgotten his name, if indeed he ever knew it. So how was he going to be found? It was this realisation that finally convinced him that he would have to go and look for the shepherd. So he swallowed his pride and set out in search of him.

I'm worried about Paul. Why? you may ask. Is he not on his way back to the flock? Yes, he is and this makes me happy. But I know what the average shepherd and the average flock are like. What worries me is this: Will he be welcomed by anyone? Will his return even be noticed?

I know there will be rejoicing in heaven at his return. But wouldn't it be nice if there was a little rejoicing on earth too?

Lost in Our Midst

Sheep get lost only in a geographical sense. When this happens, one can go and look for them. Often it is a relatively easy job to find them, especially when one knows their haunts. When found, you bring them back, and that's that.

People too get lost in the geographical sense. But they also get lost in other ways. Examples: people addicted to alcohol or drugs, people who can't settle down, people who can't hold down a job or finish a course of studies, people who are unable to maintain a stable relationship, and so on.

All of these are, in a sense, lost, and it is extremely difficult to find them. What makes it so frustrating is the fact that usually they are not far away. Often they are within arm's reach.They are lost in our midst, lost even within the bosom of the family. Yet, near and all as they are, you can't reach them.

They are like a boat without an anchor, or a sailor without a compass. Confused and lacking in motivation and will-power, they seem incapable of piloting their own frail craft. They cause enormous pain to those who care about them. And they are easy prey for the 'wolf' – the drug dealer, the unscupulous 'lover', the exploitative 'friend' …

In these cases, the task of the shepherd is not so much to find them, as to help them find themselves.

'The cruellest yearning of all is for those who are still with us.'
Helder Camara

Lost Lambs

Kevin was a smiling ten-year old. He lived with his parents and two sisters in San Francisco. One day he left his school after basketball practice. He was never seen again.

In the USA it is estimated that some 50,000 children vanish every year, of whom 5,000 are eventually found dead. Why do they go missing? Some are abducted. Some are victims of violent crimes. Some run away from unhappy homes.

Most countries have no accurate count of the number of children that go missing each year. Most police forces do not act on a report that a child is missing for at least twenty-four hours. In America the FBI say that if they were to look for every child who goes missing, they would have time for nothing else. Many countries have sophisticated programmes for tracking down stolen cars and credit cards but not for missing children.

Lord, you are the Good Shepherd who left the ninety-nine to go looking for the one that got lost, thereby showing that to you each and every one of the sheep is important and precious.

Have mercy on the human wolves who steal, exploit, and sometimes kill the lambs of the Father's flock.

Comfort the grieving parents who in many cases don't even have the consolation of a burial service.

In your merciful love grant that those lambs, though lost here, may be found hereafter.

Watch over those who are still straying here below. Guide them along paths that are safe. Send shepherds to look for them. And open the eyes of society so that we may cease to regard property as more important than people. Amen.

When the Clay Sets

Luke 16:1- 8

The Crafty Steward

The steward was unreliable, irresponsible, and dishonest. It is obvious that he had been so for quite some time. But, in spite of his craftiness, he was found out eventually, and his master confronted him with his misdeeds.

It must have been a very painful and humbling moment for him. No doubt it was also a moment of acute embarrassment for his family, if he had a family. But it was also a moment of truth and revelation, because it showed him the dishonest reality in which he had been living. Therefore, it could have been a turning point in his life. But what happened? He continued on in his old ways. There wasn't the slightest change in his character. Not the least dent in his armour.

It would seem, then, that not everybody repents. It seems that there comes a moment in our lives when the precious clay of which we are made hardens and sets, so that from that point on we can assume no new shape. To go against or change the habits of a lifetime, if not impossible, is at least extremely difficult.

The Slippery Slope

Once Michael was on a high moral plateau. Now he is on a slippery slope. What happened to him?

He worked as a bar attendant. Though his hours were bad his wages were good. It was a very busy bar. In the course of a day a lot of money went through his hands. In the beginning he was scrupulously honest. He wouldn't even take a box of matches without paying for them.

But time passed. He began to reflect on the amount of money his boss was making in a week. He reckoned that some weeks it came to thousands and to think that the boss was already a wealthy man and had his family raised, whereas he was struggling to support a wife and four kids – his being the only salary coming into the house.

So it was that he began to put his hand in the till. At first he took only a pound or two a week. Even so, his hand burned and his conscience wouldn't let him sleep at night. But gradually it became easier. The stolen money no longer burned a hole in his pocket, and his conscience quietened down.

Meanwhile he had thought up some more excellent reasons to justify his dishonesty. If he had any fear or qualm at all it was that he might be found out. He had a little stumble when a young assistant was suspected and dismissed. But it was only a hiccup. He let up for a while, then resumed again. By now his concience was sound asleep.

Footprints in the Snow

In the afternoon I went for a walk over the white fields which glistened in the sunlight. My feet sank into the soft, clean snow. For a while I walked in a kind of trance. But at a certain point I began to concentrate on the ground. It was then I noticed that the snow was full of tracks made by birds and animals. On looking attentively I was able not only to identify these birds and animals, but to tell what each was up to as well.

I saw, for instance, the scratchings of robins and sparrows in their quest for a worm. I saw the rootings of rabbits and hares looking for a blade of grass. I saw the beaten snow where sheep had passed. I saw blood on the snow where a fox had made a kill.

On a normal day you could cross and recross these fields and no matter how carefully you looked, you would see nothing of the doings of the birds and animals. Everything would be covered up. But on this day all was revealed. Their cover was blown. Everything was written there in the snow – innocence, fun, resourcefulness, pain, cunning, and red murder.

The Homing Instinct

Many birds have a powerful homing instinct. The Manx shearwater is a good example. One of these was caught and ringed in Wales. Then it was taken to Boston, three thousand miles away, where it was released. Two weeks later it was back home in Wales at the exact same spot where it was captured.

Home is not just a nest. It is a set of familiar surroundings, habits, routines, and neighbours. To have a home is to have roots. It is also to have a clear and unmistakable identity.

The homing instinct is found in humans too. People have been known to return after painful experiences, not only to their old homes, but to their old selves. They return to pick up the pieces of their former lives. Their inner selves seem hardly to have been touched. Indeed, some return enriched.

The Italian writer, Primo Levi, spent a year in Auschwitz. He was one of only three out of 123 people in his train to return. Later he said, 'If I had not been in such a place, I would perhaps be happier and more tranquil, but not so rich.' He was not, of course, talking about money.

In general the homing instinct is a positive factor. However, it can also be a negative one. The urge to return home cuts people off from new opportunities and new possibilities, and makes reform of life difficult and painful. People have been known to return from close brushes with death to lives of shallowness and mediocrity, even of crime and sin.

Whether the homing instinct is a help or a hindrance depends on where our true 'home' lies. Those who are accustomed to living in the light will return to the light. But those who are accustomed to living in the dark will, in all probability, return to the dark.

A firmly-rooted, straight tree returns to its true, upright self after the storm passes, whereas a firmly-rooted, crooked tree returns to its twisted self.

'Habit is a great deadener.' Samuel Beckett

'The best of people can become coarsened and degraded by force of habit, to the level of a beast.' Fyodor Dostoyevsky

'Habits reveal more than they conceal; they are one's true clothes.' Henry David Thoreau

'The second half of a person's life is usually made up of the habits acquired during the first half.' Fyodor Dostoyevsky

The Gate Keeper

Once upon a time there was a great kingdom. At the centre of this kingdom stood a magnificent castle. It was from this castle that the kingdom was ruled. At the time our story begins the Blues were in possession of the castle.

Robert worked for the Blues. He was in charge of the main gate leading to the castle. All who wished to enter the castle had to go through him. He wore a blue uniform which he loved dearly and kept in immaculate condition. He was both intelligent and efficient. And he was as reliable as the gateposts themselves.

Though his job was a very responsible one, it was quite straightforward. Hence, his life though busy was tranquil and uncomplicated. He knew exactly what was expected of him. He had his orders. According to those orders he was to keep out all Non-Blues.

He carried out those orders to the letter. He made not the slightest exception. He listened to no pleas, no matter how heart-rending they might be. He was especially hard on Greens. But where Blues were concerned he was the perfect gentleman, all smiles and graciousness.

Time passed. Then the Greens revolted, overthrew the Blues, and took possession of the castle. The first thing they did on coming to power was to issue a decree prohibiting all Non-Greens from entering the castle.

What happened to Robert? One might think that his head would have been one of the first to roll. Believe it or not, he retained his job. And he was every bit as faithful to his new bosses as he had been to his old ones. He was rigid in keeping out all Non-Green and, according to instructions, was especially hard on Blues. But where Green were concerned he was the perfect gentleman.

In a sense, then, the revolution scarcely touched him. In fact, there was only one tangible change in his life. He was now wearing a green uniform.

The Royal Invitation

Tom was a farmer. He was doing his spring ploughing when the king's messenger appeared unexpectedly in his field, bearing the most wonderful piece of news – he had been invited to the forthcoming royal banquet.

'Do you mean to tell me that I've been invited to the royal banquet?' he asked in disbelief.

'Yes,' the messenger replied.

On hearing this Tom began to glow like a full moon. In a flash, his humdrum life was transformed. Then, almost as an afterthought, he asked, 'By the way, when exactly is the banquet?'

'Tonight,' the messenger replied, adding, 'I'll be back in about an hour for your answer. I must have a clear yes or no.' With that the messenger left him.

The banquet was to be held that very night! This immediately changed things. He looked back at the work he had done. It was going well, very well. Then he looked ahead at what remained to be done. With luck he could finish it today. It would be a great relief to have it over with. The weather was ideal. But who could say if it would last? Then he considered the oxen. They were new to the job. He was still breaking them in. This was something which should not be interrupted.

At that moment he looked up and what did he see? He saw the royal messenger going into his neighbour's field. So that man was being invited too! Suppose, as was quite possible he was placed next to him at table? That would be not only embarrassing but also downright intolerable. All of a sudden the banquet began to lose some of its appeal.

Then there was the tedious business of getting washed and changed. And what clothes would he wear? Even his best suit was hardly good enough for a royal banquet, and he would hate to look shabby in the presence of the king and all the other guests.

Thus, one by one, the clouds of doubt began to gather, and what only a short while ago had been a blue and radiant sky, now turned murky and dark. Tom began to have second thoughts. Then third thoughts. It would be nice to finish the ploughing today. It was necessary to complete the breaking in of the oxen. 'Ah,' he sighed, 'if only the banquet was tomorrow night, and I had the ploughing done, I wouldn't think twice about accepting the invitation.'

By the time the messenger came back his mind was made up.

'Well,' said the messenger, 'are you going?'

'I have to finish this piece of ploughing,' Tom began. 'I have to finish breaking in the oxen. Besides, I ... ' But the messenger was in a hurry and interrupted him.

'Just tell me whether it is yes or no.'

'I'm afraid it will have to be no,' said Tom. He was about to resume his litany of excuses, but the messenger was already out of earshot.

The Road from Jerusalem to Jericho
Luke 10:29-37

One day a teacher announced to the class: 'Today we'll study the parable of the Good Samaritan.' Seeing a glazed look come over their eyes, the teacher asked, 'What's the matter?'

'We've heard that story many times before,' said one.

'You mean you've *listened* to the story before. But that doesn't mean you've *heard* it,' said the teacher. 'Let me ask you something. How many of you have found yourselves on that road from Jerusalem to Jericho?'

'Do you mean how many of us have been to the Holy Land?' someone asked.

'That's not what I mean,' the teacher replied.

A puzzled silence fell on the class. Then from the back of the room sobbing was heard. A this point a girl began to speak.

'I know exactly what it's like to be on that road. One day my father was driving me to the beach where we were to join the rest of the family. I was only seven at the time. It was the weekend which signals the start of the summer holidays. People were leaving the city in droves and heading for the beaches.

'As we were driving along the main highway my father suddenly got a heart attack. He managed to pull the car over to the margin where he switched off the engine. Then he asked me to try to stop a car and get help. I got out of the car and, standing ont he margin, began to wave my arms frantically at the passing motorists. At the same time I shouted as loud as I could, "Help! Help!" Hundreds of cars sped past but no one seemed to see or hear me.

'The minutes ticked away and still no one stopped. I was frightened, lonely, and desperate. Eventually, after what seemed ages, a man pulled over and stopped. I was in such a state that I was barely able to explain my plight to him. When he understood what I was saying, he immediately alerted the police. But by the time help arrived my father was already dead. He was only thirty-four years old.'

When she had finished her story the other students vented their fury on the motorists who passed by. They found it incomprehensible that so many people could ignore the cries of a desperate child. But then a fellow piped up and said, 'I can understand how it could happen.' All eyes turned in his direction as he told his story.

'Late one bitterly cold winter's night I was tired and just about to go to bed when the door bell rang. On opening the door I found a stranger standing there. He wanted a place to stay for the night. He told me he was travelling to the west. He was a student and had run out of money. He had come this far by hitch-hiking. But now that it was late he needed a place a sleep – any place, and just for the night.

'I scrutinised him up and down as he explained his predicament to me. He sounded genuine. But I felt myself getting angry with him. Why had he left it so late to seek shelter? Why handn't he planned things better? Why had he chosen to come to *my* door? Could I trust him? I continued to listen, only now I was listening more to myself than to him. From the start I more or less knew that I would not take him in.

'So out into the night I sent him, or rather left him, for I never actually took him inside at all. I closed the door firmly behind him, and watched him disappear into the cold arms of the night. Now I was *very angry* – not with him but with myself. I knew all those reasons I had lined up for refusing to take him in were nothing but flimsy, shabby excuses. I knew what the real reason was – I was just not willing to put myself out to help him.' He paused, then added, 'That's why I admire the motorist who stopped. To my mind, the likes of him are the real heroes.'

'You don't feel like a hero, nor do you want to be treated as one,' a chap interrupted at this point.

'I remember one evening I was coming home from town on my motor bike. I was coming along by the quay when I noticed a crowd looking over the river wall. I immediately guessed that someone had fallen into the river. Without stopping to analyse what I was doing, I decided to go to his aid.

'Leaving my motor bike there on the side of the street, I hurriedly threw off my coat and shoes, and dived in. However, I came up without him. Then I heard someone shout, "To your left! To your left!" Moving to my left I dived again. This time to my immense relief I found him and, with difficulty, I succeeded in bringing him to the river wall.

'At this point someone threw in a lifebelt. I secured him to it and willing hands pulled him up. By the time I had been pulled up myself, an ambulance was on the scene. Soon it was on its way to hospital. I later learned that the young man was released, apparently none the worse for his ordeal.'

A stunned silence followed. During it the eyes of all present were directed towards the rescuer. They were amazed to think that some-one so quiet was capable of such a brave deed. At a certain point the teacher brought them back to reality.

'Which of the three of your fellow students has really *heard* the story of the Good Samaritan?'

'All three of them, in different ways,' someone answered.

To Care or not to Care

Crisis does not create character, it merely reveals it. In times of cri-sis people reveal what is already inside them – the generous person or the selfish person, the hero or the coward.

When the priest, the levite, and the Samaritan came upon the man lying wounded by the side of the road, they were faced with a severe test of character, a crisis, if you like. Should they stop and help him, or should they continue about their own business? There was no es-caping the test. They had to commit themselves one way or the other. As it happened, the priest and the levite decided to pass by, while the Samaritan decided to stop and help.

What did the crisis reveal about the characters of the priest and levite? It revealed a very damning thing, namely, that they were fun-damentally self-centered persons. When the crunch came, they put their own interests first. And what did it reveal about the character of the Samaritan? A very admirable thing, namely, that he was a fundamentally unselfish person. He was the kind of man who could not pass another human being in pain without wanting to relieve that pain.

Life is continually testing us in the same way. Every day we are tested in little ways, now and again we are tested in big ways. These tests reveal the kind of people we are – fundamentally caring people, or fundamentally uncaring people. The extent of our virtue is meas-ured by our normal, usual behaviour.

'What is sin? It is to turn a deaf ear to the cries of another per-son.' Kahlil Gibran

'Of what use is a compassion that doesn't take its object into its arms?' Antoine de Saint Exupery

'The person who does a good deed is instantly enobled.' Ralph Waldo Emerson

'Few survivors feel guilty about having deliberately damaged, robbed, or beaten a companion; but by contrast, almost everybody feels guilty of having omitted to offer help ' Primo Levi writing about his experience in Auschwitz

Beatitudes for Carers

Blessed are those who care and who are not afraid to show it – they will let people know they are loved.

Blessed are those who are gentle and patient – they will help people to grow as the sun helps the buds to open and blossom.

Blessed are those who have the ability to listen – they will lighten many a burden.

Blessed are those who know how and when to let go – they will have the joy of seeing people find themselves.

Blessed are those who, when nothing can be done or said, do not walk away, but remain to provide a comforting and supportive presence – they will help the sufferer to bear the unbearable.

Blessed are those who are not afraid of sacrifice – on the day of the harvest they will sing for joy.

Blessed are those who recognise their own need to receive, and who receive with graciousness – they will be able to give all the better.

Blessed are those who give without hope of return – they will give people an experience of God.

Worlds Apart
Luke 16:19-31

Dives and Lazarus lived in different worlds. Dives was dressed in purple robes; Lazarus was dressed in rags. Dives ate splendidly every day; Lazarus didn't eat at all. Dives was healthy; Lazarus was covered with sores. Dives lived in a palace; Lazarus lived in the streets.

In fact, to say that they lived in different worlds would be an understatement. They lived in opposite worlds. Dives lived in a garden; Lazarus lived in a desert. Dives was in an earthly paradise; Lazarus in an earthly hell. And yet, though their respective worlds were as different as day and night, they lay side by side.

Lazarus was living on the very edge of Dives' world. He lay just outside his gate. Had he been somewhere else he might not have known any better. But because he was at the gate he got daily glimpses of the paradise from which he was barred. Everything he saw reminded him of what he was missing. The worst thing of all was the smell of food. It was a constant torment to him.

Though he longed to enter the world of Dives, he didn't entertain the hope of sitting at his table. He would have been blissfully happy to fill his belly with the crumbs that fell from his table. But he didn't get them. It wasn't that it couldn't be done. It was just that there was no one willing to do it. And because he was poor, there was no one to whom he could appeal, no one to put in a good word for him.

The one who was in the best position to help him was, of course, Dives. Besides the things we have already mentioned, Dives had one other thing Lazarus did not have, namely, freedom of movement. He was free to leave his comfortable world any time he wished, and so could easily have entered Lazarus' lonely, desperate world, and made contact with him. But he didn't. He had shut him out, not only of his palace, but also of his mind and heart.

People like Dives start to feel that because everything is granted to them they deserve everything, and so they don't feel the pain of those around them. They tend to acquire an ever-thicker skin in proportion to their increasing success and affluence.

Then they both died. Suddenly all was reversed. Now it was Lazarus who was sitting at the banquet table, and Dives who was locked out. Lazarus was in bliss, while Dives was in torment. It wouldn't have been quite so bad for Dives if he couldn't see the paradise in which Lazarus was now living, but he could. This meant that he knew what he was missing. And what he was missing right now was a very simple thing – water. How he pined for even a drop of it so that he might cool his burning tongue.

Back on earth, he was a man of substance and influence. When he needed something, all he had to do was ask the right person, and he immediately got what he wanted. Now he decided to try the same tactic. And so he appealed to Abraham. He asked the great man if he would send Lazarus on a mission of mercy to him. How could he appeal to the man he had ignored during his earthly life?

But the mission of mercy wasn't possible. Though Dives now desperately desired to make contact with the world of Lazarus, he could not do so. Whereas on earth their worlds lay side by side, now they were separated by a chasm, so that there was no possibility of crossing over. The time for bridge-building, for reaching out, was over.

This is a shocking parable. There is no fairy tale ending – at least not for Dives, and he is the central character in the story. We have to be careful about the people we exclude here on earth, and about the gaps we leave unbridged.

Where to Begin

One night a wealthy man had a very disturbing dream. In the dream he saw a crowd of poor, disease-ridden, starving people crying out to him for help. When he woke up the following morning, remembering his dream, he decided to embark on a crusasde of good. He wasted no time but set out in his Mercedes that very morning to see what needed to be done.

He had only just passed through the main gate of his mansion when he saw a beggarman sitting on the ground, his hand stretched out imploringly. The rich man was very upset on seeing the beggar's wretched condition. He hesitated for a moment, but then ordered his chauffer to step on the gas. He couldn't afford to stop to attend to one beggarman, no matter how wretched his condition.

He was away all day. He travelled the length and breadth of the town. He discovered that the problems were vaster, and the needs greater, than he had imagined. As he returned home in the late evening his mind was overflowing with plans, schemes, and projects. The only problem was where to begin. Should he begin with a hospital, a school, a factory, or what?

As he came to the gate of his mansion he noticed that the beggarman was still there, in the exact same position as in the morning. 'Just imagine, that poor man has been sitting there all day in the burning heat!' he said to himself. Once again a wave of pity passed over him, but once again he passed by.

That night he had another dream. Again he heard cries for help. Exept this time they were coming, not from a multitude of people, but from one individual. That individual was the beggarman he had seen at his gate. When he woke up next morning he knew exactly where to begin.

'It is not possessions which are sinful, but possessiveness, appropriating to ourselves what is not ours.' Francis of Assisi

'Without a rich heart, wealth is an ugly beggar.' Ralph Waldo Emerson

'God is ashamed when the prosperous boast of his special favour.' Rabindranath Tagore

Not Need but Greed
Luke 12:16-21

Jesus told a story about a rich farmer whose land was so productive that he had nowhere to store all the grain. So what did he do? He decided to build new and bigger barns. This done, he would sit back and enjoy life.

He set out at once to turn his dream into reality. Everything else went overboard. His one and only aim was to amass as much corn as he possibly could. But he never got to fulfil his great plan because one night he died suddenly.

What was it all for? Is the purpose of life to make ourselves rich in earthly possessions, or is it, as Jesus says, 'to make ourselves rich in the sight of God?'

One Last Grain

It wasn't that there were only a few grains of wheat scattered on the road opposite the mill. There was a whole heap of them – more than he could eat in a lifetime.

It wasn't that he hadn't eaten for days and was dying of hunger. He ate well every day, and at that moment his ample craw was bulging with grain.

It wasn't that there were flocks of birds about, all fighting him for the wheat. There were only a few nibblers – a couple of sparrows and a few wagtails. He was the only crow.

It wasn't that he was in a hurry to get to work. He had nothing to do and all day to do it.

It wasn't that the traffic was heavy. It was early morning and there was hardly anything moving.

It wasn't that he didn't see the car approaching. He did. He had a perfect view of it. Moreover, long experience enabled him to estimate accurately the speed and distance of on-coming vehicles.

So how then did he get hit?

He saw this last grain of wheat lying there. It was bigger than the others, or so it seemed to him. He was determined to have it, and have it now. Just that last one. Then he would be off.

He reached out for it. 'Ah, I've got it!' he cried, as he picked it up and gobbled it down. Then he launched himself into the air. But he was just a fraction of a second too late. The car hit him and he died in a flurry of feathers.

With the force of the impact his craw burst open so that the grains he had gathered to himself were scattered all over the road. Within seconds the little nibblers were feasting on them.

The Ambitious Executive

Once there was an executive who had a well-paying job with a thriving company. He lived with his wife and young family in a fine house in a good neighbourhood. However, he wasn't satisfied. He was young and full of energy. Anything seemed possible. He was also full of ambition. So he said to himself, 'I can do better than this. How? I'll just have to work harder.'

So he applied for overtime, of which there was no shortage. He doubled his salary. He moved to a larger house in a more fashionable part of the city. He gave his old car to his wife, and bought a sports model for himself. Even though he was doing splendidly, he still wasn't satisfied. He had his eye on a dream house but didn't yet have the money to buy it. But a few more years and he would.

He never did get to own that dream house, for he was struck down by a terminal illness. Suddenly he found himself at death's door. Then, to his horror, he discovered that he hardly knew his children, or his wife for that matter. Worse, he realised he hadn't really lived up to now. He had been postponing life until the day when all his goals would be achieved.

In the eyes of the company and of his neighbours, he was a great success. But in his own eyes he knew he had failed. He had missed out on all the important things in life. He felt empty, spiritually and emotionally. It was not the happiest state to be in now that his earthly voyage was rapidly coming to an end. Oh, how he wished he could start all over again. How differently he would do things.

'*My wealth is not possession but enjoyment.*' Henry David Thoreau

'*In the western world human fulfilment is measured by material things, so that the person who has nothing is nothing.*' Laurens van der Post

Faraway Hills

Bernard lived at the southern end of the lake. Directly opposite him lived a neighbour. Even though only six miles separated them, he had never met his neighbour. In fact, he didn't even know his name.

Bernard's cottage stood about a hundred feet from the edge of the lake. There were rhodondendrons at the front of it and pines at the back. Above the pines, a rocky hill sloped upwards to a height of several hundred feet. Here and there among the rocks gorse and heather grew.

Any way you looked at it, it was a snug little nest. When he came here ten years ago he was looking for a refuge from the city. As soon as he laid eyes on it he said, 'This is it!' He settled down at once and enjoyed a period of sweet contentment.

However, such is human nature that it tires even of the best. So it was that Bernard experienced a creeping disenchantment with his refuge. If only the cottage was a little larger. If only it was not so exposed to the bitter wind that sometimes blew across the lake from the north. If only the hill behind it was not so rugged. If only this or that was different, it would be another story.

At first he was reluctant to admit his unhappiness, much less confront it. After all, he had the house of his dreams, so he should be happy. But he wasn't. Whereas prior to this he had scarcely given his neighbour's house a glance, now in his growing unhappiness he found himself gazing at it in wonderment for what seemed like hours at a time.

What gorgeous shrubs were growing in front of it. What magnificent trees were growing behind it. What a charming hill rose up above the trees. As for the house itself! It was more like a castle, an enchanted castle at that. Sadness welled up in his heart as he gazed at it, especially when summer drew a cloak of purple haze over it. What he wouldn't give to live over there!

He reached a stage where he couldn't keep his eyes off his neighbour's house, while he couldn't bear to look at his own. Finally, one summer's evening, he decided to take a closer look at the idyllic house on the northern shore of the lake. He got into his boat and began to row across the lake. As he did so he never once looked behind him. Why should he? Was he not trying to get away from all that?

It was a perfect evening. The air was still. The surface of the lake was like glass. A smoky haze enveloped everything, making it impossible to see objects clearly but investing them with an air of magic and enchantment. He felt excitement mount inside him.

However, as he made his way across the lake, a strange thing happened. The veil of haze gradually lifted. Ever so slowly objects came into focus. Blurred edges became clearly defined. Things assumed their true shape and donned their natural colours. At a certain point the veil disappeared altogether so that for the first time he was able to get a clear view of his neighbour's house. To his amazement it appeared quite ordinary.

He was bitterly disappointed. All of a sudden the excitement went out of the journey, and he felt like turning around and heading straight back home. However, after a moment of deep uncertainty, he decided that having come this far he might as well go all the way across. By now the sun had disappeared so that he found himself rowing into deepening shadow.

On reaching the shore he disembarked. Then he stood there for several minutes looking around him. He could scarcely believe his eyes. The house was only a cottage after all, a cottage similar in many respects to his own. The shrubs were rhododendrons. The trees pines. And the hill behind the cottage was if anything even more rugged than his own hill. All the magic had evaporated. All the enchantment had fled. The castle was an illusion. He felt not only disappointed but foolish as well.

Well, now that he had seen what it was really like, he had no intention of hanging around the place. He was about to get into the boat when he suddenly heard a voice say, 'Hello there!' It was his neighbour.

'Jack's the name,' his neighbour said extending his hand.

'My name is Bernard,' he answered. 'I live on the far side of the lake.'

They began to chat. After a while Jack said, 'By the way, that's a beautiful house you've got over there.'

'What house are you talking about?' Bernard asked absent

'That house over there,' Jack replied, pointing across the lake. 'That's your house, isn't it?'

For the first time that evening Bernard looked backwards. Over there the sun was still shining, tinging the hills with gold. He let his eyes roam all over those hills. Finally they came to rest on his own cottage.

'You're right!' he suddenly exclaimed. 'It is a beautiful house.'

'It is more like a magic kingdom, if you ask me,' Jack added.

Bernard felt his heart beating rapidly. Transfixed with joy, he stood there gazing across at his cottage. Finally Jack cut in on his reverie and said, 'It's getting late. Maybe you should be getting back?'

'I should,' said Bernard. Then shaking hands warmly he said, 'So long for now. We must get better acquainted.'

He set out for home with a light heart.

Taking Care of Our Gifts
Matthew 25:14-30

Our True Birth Place

A talent has first of all to be discovered and recognised. How many lovely things are waiting to be found and recognised – flowers in the forest, treasure under the sea, talents hidden in people. It is sad when a talent is not recognised by others. It is even sadder when it is not recognised by its possessor. It has been said that our true birthplace is the place in which we awaken to our gifts and talents.

After a talent has been recognised comes the task of developing it. Every talent, even the most instinctive, has to be practised in order to be made perfect. Taking care of the gifts we have received is not the same as keeping them in a vault. Again it is sad to see a talent allowed to go to waste, or when its possessor is not given the opportunity of exercising it.

Some talents wither and die if left undeveloped and unused. Penguins have wings yet they cannot fly. Why is this? Is it that they once could fly but didn't, and so in time lost the ability? Even when a talent is recognised and developed, a lot of hard work, discipline, and patience are required if it is to bear its full fruit. Outsiders looking in do not always understand this, as Patrick Kavanagh tells us:

> I have not the fine audacity of men
> Who have mastered the pen
> Or the purse.
> The complexes of many slaves are in my verse.
> When I straighten my shoulders to look at the world boldly
> I see talent coldly
> Damning me to stooped attrition.
> Mine was a beggar's mission
> To dreams of beauty I should have been born blind.
>
> I should have been content to walk behind

Watching the reflection of God's delight:
A secondhand teller of the story
A secondhand glory.
It was not right
That my mind should have echoed life's overtones
That I should have seen a flower
Petalled in mighty power.

The Complete Poems of Patrick Kavanagh, 1984, Newbridge, The Goldsmith Press, p. 59.

A Born Footballer?

I don't believe there is any such thing as a born footballer, or writer, or painter. But Paul came very close to being an exception. He was a star footballer. He did, of course, have to work at it as a youngster. Still, everybody agreed he was a natural. He had it, and had it right from the beginning. Moreover, he knew it. He had an inborn confidence in his own ability. He knew he was better than any of the kids around him.

It came as no surprise when at fifteen he was snapped up by a leading First Division club. He didn't have long to wait for his big chance. He had only just celebrated his sixteenth birthday when he found himself selected for the first team. He grabbed his opportunity with both hands. He made an immediate impact and kept his place on the team. Almost overnight he shot from obscurity to fame.

From there on it was one success after another. Within two years he was the club's leading scorer. By now he was also playing for his country. Everywhere football was talked about his name was mentioned. To the fans he was a hero. To the media he was a celebrity.

He revelled in his success. He had come a long way in a very short time. A few years ago he was a poor kid playing in the back streets of a provincial town. Now he was not only famous but rich as well. He married a beautiful model, drove a Mercedes, and was the envy of every schoolboy who played football.

Soon, however, things started to go wrong, and the bright lights began to grow dim. There were rumours that he was drinking, drinking heavily. The rumours proved to be well founded. His football began to suffer. His personal life began to grow ragged. His wife suddenly left him. She claimed that he was immature, selfish, and irresponsible.

Sadly, Paul's glittering career came to a premature end. He was remembered as much for the manner in which he squandered a rare talent as for anything he achieved with it. Of what use is it to develop one's talent if one leaves oneself undeveloped?

Beware of that talent which springs up overnight with little or no effort on your part. Better that it should grow up with you, quietly and almost unnoticed, like a seed grows into a tree. When a talent grows up from below and from within, a kind of wholeness results.

The Most Talented People of All

For forty arduous years Moses led the people of God through the desert towards the promised land. He brought them through hunger and thirst, heat and cold, snakes, fear and despair. And what did he get from them in return? Complaints, grumbling, lack of cooperation. And just when the end of this tortuous journey was in sight, death suddenly appeared at the door of his tent.

However, God smiled on him. He led him up the slopes of Mount Nebo. From the top Moses looked across the river Jordan at the land of promise. As he let his eyes roam over it, his heart thrilled with joy. He saw that it was indeed a land of streams and springs, a land of wheat and barley, a land flowing with milk and honey.

Yet, in his heart of hearts, he knew he himself would not eat that bread, or drink that milk, or taste that honey. Nevertheless, he was happy. He had fulfilled himself by leading his people to the enjoyment of these things.

Just as the sun helps to bring to birth the fragrant flowers that lie hidden in the soil of the fields, so there are people who find their fulfilment in helping to unfold the talents God has deposited in others, thus enabling them to enter a land they themselves will never enter. Perhaps these are the most talented people of all.

What Have I Made of Myself?

When Christ was talking about talents, we must not think he was thinking about a musical talent or a footballing talent. Such talents are important, and all credit to those who possess them, develop them, and use them well. But they are outrageously over-valued and over-rewarded in our times. Christ's parable goes a lot deeper. Each of us could say, 'I am the talent.' Hence, the all-important question is: What have I made of myself?

'Some people refuse to believe in my existence,' the voice began. 'I don't blame them since my public appearances are so few and fleeting. Even you doubt my existence. Now you ought to know better. You ought to know that I do exist, and that I'm absolutely real. But just look at the way you treat me. You keep me chained up as if I were a mad dog. You keep me under wrappers as if I were a piece of rare china. You keep me out of sight as if I were something to be ashamed of.'

'Oh, but I do take you out,' I protested.

'Yes, you do,' the voice replied. 'I was exaggerating a little when I said you never take me out. But you take me out so seldom that I can't bear the light, and I'm crippled from living in cramped quarters. You take me out on special occasions, and even though I give you great pleasure, and bring joy to your guests, when the feast is over you wrap me up carefully, surround me with mothballs, and hide me away once more. In ordinary times the best I can hope for is to be taken out now and then for a little dusting and airing.'

'Who are you?' I asked anxiously.

'I am your better self, crying for recognition,' came the reply.

Finding One's Element

How miserable the seal looked as he lay on the flat rocks – a gigantic blob of useless fat and shapeless flesh. He was not so much living as languishing, without energy or spirit, a pathetic creature that inspired pity rather than admiration. But the fact was, the poor fellow was simply out of his element.

Then I watched as he began to manoeuvre himself towards the sea by means of slow, laborious, cumbersome movements which were painful to watch. But once he hit the water he was transformed. He became another creature – sleek, beautiful, totally at ease. Then he proceeded to accomplish with effortless skill such a variety of complicated movements that it was a joy to watch him. He was now in his element.

People, too, need to find their element if they are to be seen at their best. Wonderful things happen when people do the thing for which they were destined.

'I have no special gift; I am only passionately curious.' Albert Einstein

'It's not what an artist does that counts, but what he is.' Pablo Picasso

'There is no divine grace to absolve us from the process of becoming.' Antoine de Saint Exupery

The Race
Matthew 20:1-16

The kingdom of heaven is like a race in which there were several runners. The runners stayed bunched together until the last lap. Halfway round this, the eventual winner eased himself into the lead. As he did so another man fell back into last place after a desperate but vain effort to keep up. The other runners were strung out between those two extremities.

As the leader came into the home straight, the crowd rose to him. Sensing that a record was on, the people roared their encouragement. When the news was flashed up that the winner had broken the record, thunderous applause echoed around the stadium. The cameras followed him as he did a lap of honour. He got a standing ovation as he went around. People waved flags in a delirium of joy. Here and there bouquets of flowers were thrown in his direction.

When he finished the lap he was mobbed. Everybody wanted to clap him on the back and shake his hand. People fought to get his autograph. Microphones were thrust in front of him. 'How does it feel to be a champion?' he was asked. Beaming all over he replied, 'Wonderful! Absolutely wonderful!' Already newspapers were queueing up for the exclusive rights to his story, and company executives, cheque books in hand, were doing likewise for the right to use his name to endorse their products.

While all this was going on, the other runners had finished the race. The last man really had to struggle to finish. In fact, he collapsed as he crossed the line. However, there was no one at hand to raise him up. Having rested for a while, he picked himself up and, with head bowed, departed for the dressing rooms.

A VIP had been invited to perform the prize-giving ceremony. The first three runners home were waiting, all smiles, to take their places on the victory podium. All eyes were fixed on them. The first sign that something unusual was about to happen was when the VIP said he wanted all the runners present at the ceremony. What a nice touch! the organisers thought. The runners were duly called, and all was now set.

Then what did he do? He called forth the man who came in last and gave the gold medal to him. He gave the silver medal to the man who had come second last, and the bronze medal to the man who came third last. There were gasps of astonishment from the crowd, and sighs of embarrassment from the organisers. The mistake was politely but firmly pointed out to him. But, with equal politeness and firmness, he said, 'There has been no mistake. This is the way I want it.' Then he proceeded to give a warm handshake to each of the other runners right down to the man who came first. When the latter came forward he was very angry.

'This is not fair' he exclaimed.

'So you think it's not fair?' the VIP replied calmly.

'No,' said the man. 'I won the race. I deserve to get the gold medal.'

'Friend,' said the VIP, 'haven't you got enough already?'

'What do you mean?' the man asked.

'Well, first and foremost, you've had the satisfaction of winning the race. Then you've had the applause of the crowd and the attention of the media. On top of all this, you've had lucrative contracts offered to you. Now consider the man who came in last. He finished the race too, and it cost him every bit as much as it cost you. And what did he get for his efforts? Nothing. Absolutely nothing. Would it be fairer if you got everything while he got nothing?'

With that the victor was reduced to silence. Still fuming, he turned and went away.

Like Christ's story of the labourers in the vineyard (Matthew 20:1-16) this is, strictly speaking, an unfair story. But which of us would like to be treated by God according to strict justice?

Labourers by the Roadside

One day while in Cape Town, South Africa, I saw Christ's parable re-enacted before my eyes – well, at least part of it. I saw a large number of men at the crossroads on the edge of a shanty town. Some of them were lying there. But could you blame them with the sun blazing down on them? However most of them were standing. No doubt they figured they had a better chance that way.

What were they doing there? They were engaged in that most humbling of occupations – waiting. They were waiting for some farmer or builder to come along and hire them for the day. Some had been there since sunrise. Indeed I was told that some of them had been there overnight. And still you will find people who say that these people do not want to work.

They were totally exposed. They were on view, on display. Many eyes scan them – indifferent eyes, curious eyes, even hostile eyes. Their value depends on what people want from them. They have no value in themselves. They will settle for practically any wage – whatever the hirer is willing to pay. It is already ten o'clock in the morning. A look of dejection is beginning to settle on their faces. The day is wearing on. Hope is fading.

Here, I'm afraid, is where the similarity with Christ's parable ends. For most of these men there will be no happy ending. There will be no eleventh hour reprieve. They will go home to their shacks and their families empty-handed.

In this world the first shall be first, and the last shall be last.

'Do we not all secretly long for more love than reason, more pardon than justice, more impulse than calculation, more heart than head?' Laurens van der Post

'Our civilisation is in danger because we value people more for the use we can make of them than for what they are in themselves.' Laurens van der Post

The Man Who Was out on a Limb
Luke 19:1-10

Zacchaeus must have known that he didn't belong there since his lifestyle was in complete opposition to everything Jesus stood for. Why then did he show up at all? The Gospel says he was anxious to see what Jesus looked like. I suspect there was a deeper reason. It must have been that the wick of goodness still smouldered in his heart.

He didn't join the crowd. He climbed up among the branches of a sycamore tree. In more ways that one, he was out on a limb. He was marginalised, not by poverty, but by riches. His riches, while insulating him against the hardships of life, isolated him from his fellow townspeople who, by and large, were poor.

The searching eye of Jesus spotted him on the tree, that attentive, caring eye which had spotted Nathanael sitting under the fig tree (John 1:48). Even though the Good Shepherd was surrounded by a noisy crowd, he kept his eyes open for the sheep on the margins of the flock. He didn't allow himself to get carried away by the wave of adulation.

He stopped under the tree and looked up at Zacchaeus. The people looked up too and saw Zacchaeus sitting there. No doubt they expected and hoped that Jesus would give him a thorough dressing down. Had he done so he would have enhanced his popularity in the town.

But Jesus did not do the expected. He refused to read the riot act to Zacchaeus. He did not extinguish the smouldering wick. Instead, he did something which made him immediately unpopular with the people. He asked Zacchaeus if he could dine in his house, and surprisingly Zacchaeus received him with joy.

Zacchaeus was a bit like a man who knows there is something the matter with him but hasn't the courage to go and see a doctor. However, when a kindly doctor comes unexpectedly to his door, he is relieved, and welcomes him.

Jesus left the others there complaining, 'He has gone to stay at a sinner's house', and went off to devote his full attention to the one who was lost. Everybody knew Zacchaeus was a scoundrel, and obviously thought he was beyond redemption. However, I suspect that the real reason why they were mad with Jesus was not that they thought Zacchaeus was beyond redemption, but that he didn't deserve it. They didn't want to see him saved. They wanted to see him condemned and punished.

But Jesus didn't think like this. He saw that Zacchaeus was in desperate need of salvation. There was no question of whether or not he was deserving of it. He needed it – that was enough.

Zacchaeus had come in order to see what kind of man Jesus was. Well, by the end of the day he had got a lot more than he bargained or hoped for. Instead of getting a mere passing glimpse of Jesus, he had a face to face, and a heart to heart encounter with him. He not only discovered what Jesus looked like but also what his heart was like. And to know the heart of Jesus was to know the possibilities of his own heart too. Zacchaeus liked what he discovered about himself. His heart burst into life like a desert landscape after rainfall.

From Spectator to Participant

Thanks largely to television, we live in the age of the spectator, the onlooker, the bystander. Take nature lovers. Now they don't have to get their shoes dirty, or let the rain fall on them. They don't even have to leave their own sitting rooms, or soft chairs, or even move from the fireside. Television serves up to them a feast of sights and sounds, on a plate, as it were.

But what a poor substitute this is for the real thing. True, there is no risk, no pain, no trouble. But it is only a shadow compared to the real thing. We have people who claim to love nature who seldom if ever have walked in the woods, across the fields, or along the shore. In other words, they are mere spectators. They are not really involved. To be involved is to give a part of oneself to it. But what one gets back far outweighs what one gives.

However, there is at least this to be said for the spectator – he or she is interested. And where there is interest, there is the possibility of a real involvement.

So it was with Zacchaeus. At the start of the story he was a mere spectator. He had found an ideal vantage point – a sycamore tree. Thanks to its large leaves, he could see without being seen. But he wasn't part of what was happening on the ground. He was just an onlooker.

As an onlooker he was involved only passively. He was there on his own terms. There was a certain interest, but no risks, no commitment. When it was over he could go home, weigh up the pros and cons, and then decide to take it further or drop it.

But what happened? Jesus saw him and invited him to become a participant. Suddenly Zacchaeus was whisked from the touchline right into the centre of the action. He was like a spectator who goes to a football game, and suddenly the manager spots him, throws him a set of gear, and says, 'You're on!' And he finds himself playing.

The amazing thing is this. Not only did Zacchaeus respond positively, but he did so immediately and joyfully. There is joy in watching, but there is far more joy in participating. The consequences for him were enormous. It changed his life.

Antoine de Saint Exupery was a pilot. In the early days of World War II he volunteered to fly reconnaissance missions over France to monitor the advance of the German army. He wrote to a friend:

> Mud. Rain. Rheumatism in a farmhouse. Empty evenings. The melancholy of doubt. Anxiety at 35,000 feet. Fear also, of course. Everything that is demanded of a man in order to be a man among men. And I'm united with my fellow men, because if I separated myself from them, I'm nothing. How I despise spectators. (From *Wartime Writings*, p.18)

Right Approach

In trying to correct people, the kind of approach we adopt is all-important. If we approach people only to confront them with their faults, in all probability we will achieve nothing. In fact, we may only make matters worse. They are likely to close up, become resentful, and harden their attitudes.

But if we adopt the approach Jesus used with Zacchaeus, that is, ask them to do something for us, the miracle of change can happen. Through this approach we show them that we believe in them, that we have confidence in them. The result is that they drop their guard and open up. Once they open up anything can happen.

In from the Cold

As soon as the youth entered the compartment the passengers already there took an instant dislike to him. They didn't like the sour look on his unshaven face. They didn't like the clothes he wore. They didn't like his hairstyle. They didn't like the way he barged into the compartment, their compartment. They saw to it that he occupied the seat furthest from them, a corner seat. They made not the slightest effort to include him in their conversation.

The youth got the message. He knew they didn't want him. So he turned away and spent his time gazing silently out the train window. The look on his face became sourer with each milestone that flashed past.

Then an elderly, dignified looking lady entered the compartment. Without hesitating for as much as a second she sat down in the seat opposite him. He turned and threw a gloomy glance in her direction. She noticed it at once and smiled. He hesitated, then nodded faintly. She smiled again. The ice was broken. He was in from the cold.

They began to talk. Then he noticed that she had left a bag on the floor. He offered to find room for it on the overhead rack. When he had done so she thanked him, and they continued to chat. As they chatted, from time to time he was heard to laugh out loud and she to chuckle. She exuded charm and kindness. He felt that she not only accepted him but actually liked him as well. Gradually his whole demeanour and manner changed. He became almost a different person. It was clear that beneath a rugged exterior there lay no small capacity for gentleness. You never improve people by rejecting them.

Turning One's Life Around
Luke 7:36-50

Mary knew she was on a downward path. She knew she was sinking deeper and deeper into the mire, getting further and further into the dark forest. It was no easy path she was on. She was covered in mud, scratches, bruises, and cuts. She was severely undernourished from eating worthless fruit.

How come, then, she kept going on and on, hopelessly, blindly, recklessly? There was a kind of cold comfort in staying where she was. But of course she could not stay where she was; she was daily being carried further into the darkness.

She knew that a decision awaited her. She longed to be able to make that decision, but kept postponing it. She was hoping for a miracle – that the sky might open above her, and a friendly hand reach down to pluck her out of the swamp, or that the forest would open up before her, and she would find her way out of it quickly and painlessly.

Eventually she faced the fact that it was futile to wait for a miracle. She would have to turn around and face back all the way she had come. It called for no little courage simply to face the truth of her condition. It called for humility to admit her mistakes and to take responsibility for them. It would require great strength to undertake the long journey back. She knew it would be painful, even though she was convinced it would lead to a better life.

It was his arrival in town that gave her the courage to begin the journey back. She appeared before him just as she was. The others looked at her and saw the 'mud'. Jesus looked at her and saw the wounds. He saw that she had been sufficiently judged and punished by life. What she needed was healing, not condemnation. Therefore, he received her with compassion.

From that day a new world opened up in front of her. She began to live a new life. However, she would not be reborn immediately.

She had only just been plucked from the swamp. The mud still clung to her, and would continue to do so for some time to come.

There is no such thing as an instant and painless recovery from illnesses of the soul and the spirit. One has to suffer in order to recover. This may sound like a contradiction. The following illustration will help to show that this is not so.

Suppose you are out on a very cold day and your feet become numb. Then you come inside and place them in a basin of hot water. At first you feel nothing. But they begin to thaw out gradually. As they do so, you begin to feel the heat of the water, a heat which causes you to experience a scalding pain. It is when you begin to feel this pain that you know your legs are coming back to normal. So, when you begin to feel pain, know that you are getting well. But for this very reason the idea of recovery can be terrifying.

Mary was on that new path which her deeper self always wanted to travel. She would travel further down it than any of those who were now judging her. By welcoming her as he did, and graciously accepting her gift, Jesus put wind in her sails.

Dagger for a Wounded Heart

I heard the following story from a white man in Cape Town, South Africa.

'The area into which I had recently moved was crawling with loiterers. The loiterers had one thing in common. They were coloured, that is, of mixed race. You could see them hanging around, staring into homes and gardens. I immediately assumed they were up to mischief. But in at least one case I was way off the mark.

'I should have known better. The looks on their faces should have alerted me. Their eyes seemed to caress objects, not to covet them. But it was not until later that I realised this. I had forgotten something. Not too long ago this had been a coloured area, but the people had been evicted by the government and scattered to different parts of the city.

'One evening on arriving home from work I spotted a coloured man looking into my garden. I couldn't imagine what he was looking at, for there was hardly anything in the garden apart from an old pear tree. My indignation flared up. So, in an extremely angry mood, I went out and confronted him.

'"What are you doing here?" I demanded.

'"I grew up in this house," the man replied in an apologetic voice. "I came around to take a look at the pear tree. Some years it used to produce only a few pears. But other years it produced a lot. I just wanted to see how many pears were on it this year."

'On hearing this I felt deeply ashamed. In a flash all my anger evaporated. In a mumbling, fumbling way I tried to apologise to him, but he was already making his way down the street.

'Oh, how I regretted not having adopted a gentler approach with him. In a thoughtless and selfish way I had driven a dagger into an already deeply-wounded heart.'

To Know the Story Is to Understand

I looked at the cactus as it stood in its greenhouse pot. What immediately caught my eye was it's crude skin and formidable battery of sharp needles. These two features gave the cactus a decidedly unfriendly appearance.

'What an unsociable little fellow!' I said to myself.

But then a voice inside me said, 'Wait a minute. Before you judge him, you've got to know where he comes from. You've got to hear his story. Then maybe you will understand. him, and when you understand him, you won't be so eager to judge him.

'This little chap grew up in a very harsh environment. Right from infancy, while most other flowers were basking in the sun and dancing in the wind, he was fighting just to stay alive. The desert is a very hostile place, you know.

'See that tough skin. Well, without that he would not have been able to withstand the burning rays of the sun. Without that he would have shrivelled up because he would have no moisture in him.

'And see those needles. Well, water is the most precious commodity in the desert. The cactus, being able to conserve water, is a natural target for the animals. These are only too willing to give him a good squeeze, not alas out of love, but to extract the water he contains. Naturally, the cactus has to defend himself. This is where the needles come in. Once the animals make contact with these, they quickly get the point.'

The inner voice fell silent.

I looked again at the cactus. Now I no longer saw the rough skin and sharp needles. The thing that immediately caught my eye was the exquisite flower growing right out of its heart.

All of a sudden I was filled with admiration for the little cactus which, in spite of the hardships and difficulties, was still able and willing to offer to the world the treasures of its heart.

The Transformation

As I passed the old cherry tree in February, it had a bare and forlorn look about lt. It contained not a shred of beauty. It was doing absolutely nothing to relieve the unrelenting drabness of winter's all-embracing overcoat. In fact, it required no small act of faith to believe that it was still alive.

I passed the tree again in April. When I looked at it I could scarcely believe my eyes, so great was the transformation it had undergone in that short interval of time. It was now decked out in a robe of brilliant blossoms which filled the air with fragrance and caused the surrounding scene to explode with colour. Two months ago it looked like a corpse; now it was an eloquent witness to life.

'From where has all this beauty come?' I asked myself.

Could it by chance have fallen out of the sky and alighted on the tree? Or had someone waved a magic wand over it? Nothing of the kind. All this newness, freshness and fragrance; all these buds, blossoms and shoots had come from within the tree itself! On looking at it back in February, when it was still in the grip of winter, who could have believed that it contained all this?

Sometimes on the evidence of perhaps only one encounter, we write off people as having no possibilities. We do those people a great injustice. Every human being is a well of possibilities. If in some people these possibilities have not yet manifested themselves, all it means is that for them spring has not yet come.

'Illnesses of the spirit come in on horseback but leave on foot.' Francis de Sales

'It will seem early the moment we begin in the right way.' Henry David Thoreau

'It is when the fall is lowest that charity ought to be the greatest.' Victor Hugo

'If you want to find the spark, you must look among the ashes.' Elie Wiesel

'He who loves good is indulgent towards evil.' Antoine de Saint Exupery

Choosing the Better Part

Jesus said to Martha, 'You worry and fret about so many things, and yet few are needed, indeed only one. It is Mary who has chosen the better part.' (Luke 10:38-42)

Many of the things that go to make up our daily round are urgent and important in their own way. But few could truly be called essential. We have to learn to distinguish between the two. Like Martha, I'm afraid that many times we give priority to the urgent. The essential, the one thing necessary, gets postponed until later, when, if it is done at all, it is done hurriedly and badly.

Therefore, we have to look beyond the daily chores and urgencies. We have to take time out for reflection. Otherwise we run the risk of living like ants which don't seem to be happy unless they are rushing around with loads on their backs.

'Prime time' is the most valuable time on television. How often do we give prime time to God?

'I blame not the priority you give to things of daily need; but for making them your end.' Antoine de Saint Exupery

• • •

Jesus came to the house of Martha and Mary. Whereas Martha busied herself with the details of hospitality, Mary sat down at his feet and listened to him. Mary was a good listener; Martha was not.

It's not easy to be a good listener. If we want to listen well, the first thing we have to do is stop what we're doing – turn off the television, put down the newspaper, stop drying the dishes – so that we can give our undivided attention to the speaker. We have to give up some of our precious time. This is easier said than done when, like Martha, we have a lot of things to do and no one to help us, or when we are tired and just want to be left alone.

The second thing we have to do is stop talking. This is even more difficult. Often we talk so as to defend ourselves from the truth. We interrupt, counter, object, to keep the message from encroaching. To be silent is to drop our defences, and allow the message to enter.

Those who cannot listen cannot learn. When the Lord left, Martha was none the richer for his coming. She had allowed the word of God to fall among thorns. Mary on the other hand had made sure that this most precious of all seeds fell on good soil.

• • •

It's terrible to be all alone on the road of life. Hence the importance of friends. Jesus had three friends in Bethany – Martha, Mary, and Lazarus. He loved them and they loved him. He knew he could rely on them, and they knew they could rely on him. Friendship is not like a flower which blooms in summer and withers in winter.

Hence, when other doors were being closed against him, he went to their door, and found an oasis of hospitality and peace. And when Lazarus died, the sisters turned to him, and found comfort, hope, and life.

We all need at least one person with whom we can be instinctively transparent, someone with whom we can be completely ourselves, and therefore totally at peace. Whenever friendly paths meet, the whole world becomes like home.

• • •

The Lord was coming to my house. So I scrubbed it from top to bottom, cleaning and polishing everything. Then I laid the table with the best tablecloth, best set of delph, best silverware, and so on. I put candles and flowers there too. When all was ready and my guest was about to arrive, I rolled out the red carpet.

He came and I think I did him proud. I waited on him hand and foot. No king ever had such service lavished on him. I made sure that the conversation never flagged. He, for his part, was most gracious. He showed so much appreciation that I was embarrassed. When he left I felt real good, and yet something was bothering me.

For a while I was at a loss as to what this was. Then a question arose within me: What did he want from me? Food? Hospitality? I wondered. But then I heard a second question sounding inside me: What was it that he wanted to give me? I felt sure that he wanted to give me something. But, whatever it was, I gave him no opportunity of giving it to me.

Anointed with Love

John 12:1-8

Mary wanted to thank Jesus. She needed to show her appreciation, and had an excellent reason for doing so – he had raised her brother Lazarus from the dead.

But 300 denarii worth of ointment! Surely that was going a bit too far? A denarius was an average day's wage at that time. So we're talking about a whole year's wages. Surely, then, Judas had a point when he objected. Moreover, we know that Jesus came (we have his own word for it), not to have service done to him, but to serve everyone, especially the poor.

Therefore, you would have expected him to agree with Judas, notwithstanding the latter's vile motives. You would have expected him to call a halt to Mary's extravaganza, or at least to refuse it politely, saying something like, 'Oh, you don't have to do this.' But surprise! surprise! he accepted her gift, and said to Judas, 'Leave her alone.'

Amidst the growing hostility of the religious leaders, he needed her act of generosity and love. It was as welcome as a cup of cold water is to a weary desert traveller. He also implied that he needed that ointment for another reason – he was soon to die. Thus, Mary's act took on an added and deeper significance, one which she herself didn't grasp at the time – it became an advance anointing of his body in preparation for burial.

Judas sounded so reasonable and so concerned. Many people have very generous and noble ideas as to how the money of others should be spent. But it is always the money of others, never their own money.

The Birthday Party

Mrs Tynan had spent most of the previous year in a hospice for patients with terminal cancer. The doctors reckoned she had at most three months to live. Though no one had told her how close to death she was, they figured she knew. Indeed she did. Yet she was in no way morbid about it. But she wasn't exactly over the moon either – not yet at any rate.

Though she was apparently quite well-off, she was a very ordinary, simple person. She had never married. Her closest relative was a cousin who rarely came to see her.

Her seventy-fifth birthday was fast approaching. Everybody knew it would be her last. Accordingly, some of her friends got together and decided to organise a surprise party for her. They set out to make it something very special. Everybody who was anybody in her life was invited, including the cousin, of course.

When the big day finally dawned, the nurses got her up a little earlier than usual. They did her hair up neatly and dressed her in a bright new dress. When the invited guests crowded into her room, they found her sitting in a special chair. Everybody hugged and kissed her. They showered cards and presents on her. She was completely overwhelmed.

A lot of good-natured chatter followed, punctuated by bursts of loud laughter. Presently a trolley with a tray on it was wheeled in. On the tray was a large cake decked out with a host of flickering candles. Also there was a large bottle of the finest champagne. They sang 'Happy Birthday' with great gusto. Then they gave her a knife and she cut the cake. The cake was distributed and the glasses filled. Then, raising their glasses, they clinked them with hers, and drank to her health and happiness.

More songs were sung. More jokes were told. The room echoed with laughter. Everybody joined in the merriment – everybody but her serious-looking cousin who all this time remained standing outside the room, refusing to take part in the celebration. They urged him to join in, but he said,

'It's all a waste of money. Besides, it's not right. It's nothing but a big deception. Everybody knows she's dying. It's no time for laughing and joking. The way you people are carrying on inside there, you'd think she had won the lottery or something.'

He paused. Then his face grew even more serious and he added, 'And to think she hasn't even made a will yet!'

However, while he was saying all this, Mrs Tynan, with tears of happiness running down her face, was saying, 'I never knew something like this could happen to me. This is the best birthday I've ever had. This is the happiest day of my life.'

Giving and Receiving

There are some people who are very good at giving but extremely poor at receiving. It is very hard to give to give them anything, almost impossible to do them a favour. Now while such people may appear to be very generous, in reality they are extremely self-centered.

Self-centered people hate to receive. Why is this? Because it makes them feel inferior to others and puts them in debt to others. On the other hand, they love to give because it inflates their ego, thereby (unconsiously perhaps) making them feel superior to others.

But we need to receive from others. This is a statement of fact. None of us is self-sufficient. All of us are incomplete. We need to receive from one another and above all from God. It's nothing less than tragic not to be able to receive. Therefore, it is not enough to know how to give. We must also know how to receive. Both are graced activities. We could sum it up by saying: to live, we need to receive; to grow, we need to give.

Moreover, if we reject a kindness from a well-meaning person, we hurt and wound that person. We make him or her feel unappreciated and useless – as having nothing to offer. Imagine how Mary would have felt if Jesus had spurned her offering. Those who cannot receive stifle others. To receive with humility and graciousness does wonders for the giver. It makes him or her feel appreciated, and calls forth further generosity. You can't give unless there is someone to receive.

There is a difference between *accepting* a gift and *receiving* it. One can accept a kindness or favour from another as an adult accepts a gift from a child. The adult doesn't really need or want it. So what does he do? He accepts it, but when the child's back is turned, he puts it away.

To receive, as opposed to merely accept a gift, is to acknowledge one's need of the offered gift. The soil doesn't merely accept the seed; it receives it, knowing that without it, it would be barren. To receive like this is to give a gift in return. Unless the soil received the seed, the seed would not be able to multiply. There is a mutual enrichment.

Reversing Roles

During the last supper Jesus rose from table, removed his outer garment and, taking a towel, wrapped it round his waist. Then he poured water into a basin and began to wash the feet of the apostles, and to dry them with the towel. The apostles didn't understand why he was doing this. Peter objected to it, insisting that it wasn't right, and did his best to stop it happening to him.

When Jesus had finished he explained the reason for his extraordinary action. 'You call me Master and Lord, and rightly; so I am. If I, then, the Lord and Master, have washed your feet, you should wash each other's feet. I have given you an example so that you may copy what I have done. Happiness will be yours if you behave accordingly.' (John 13:13-15.17)

He was teaching them a lesson – that for them authority was to be a form of service. No one should be allowed to rule who hadn't proved that he could serve.

Today there is often a gulf between those who serve and those who are served, between those who rule and those who are ruled. A lot of misunderstanding and hurt results especially for those below. Those in low positions often feel they are neither understood nor appreciated by those in high positions. They see the latter as remote and uncaring.

How easy it is for those who have worked their way up into high positions to forget what it is like to be 'in the trenches'. They may say glibly, 'It's tough at the top.' The truth is – it's a lot tougher at the bottom.

The gulf between those above and those below also leads to a lot of harsh judgements being handed down. When we ourselves are the victims of such judgements, it makes us hate all judgements as unfair and unhelpful.

Would that those above might follow the example Jesus gave at the last supper. Let the policeman be arrested; the priest sit in the pew; the teacher sit at the desk; the foreman get down into the trenches; the warder be locked up; the doctor get seriously ill; the judge be put in the dock; the general go to the front line; the man with the secure job join the dole queue ... Might we not have a more just, caring, and sensitive exercise of authority?

The Watch and the Clock

Of course the opposite also happens – those above are not understood by those below, and harsh judgements are sometimes handed up.

One day a watch was crossing the town square just as the big clock on the church steeple was tolling twelve noon. The watch looked up at the big clock and said,

'You think you're better than the rest of us, don't you? You spend your time looking down on everybody. You ought to take a good look at yourself. Your face is so common, your hands so clumsy, and your voice so coarse!'

But the big clock calmly replied, 'Come up here, my little brother, and I'll show you something.'

With that the little watch climbed up the unending stairs, and at last stood beside the big clock. It was even bigger from close up. What a view there was from here. But pretty soon it began to see things differently. It was dangerous up here, very exposed, and ever so lonely.

'Little brother, there is a man down there who wants to know the time. Why don't you tell him?' said the big clock.

'Oh, I couldn't make him hear me from here or see me either,' the watch replied.

'I see,' said the big clock. 'So you can't tell him. But I can tell him. We each have a job to do. I can do what you can't do. You can do what I can't do. Let us therefore not criticise one another. Instead let each of us in our own way, and from our own place, tell people the time. In that way, we will not only be equal but brothers as well.'

Letting Go

During the same supper Jesus began to talk about leaving. Not surprisingly, the apostles were plunged into gloom at the prospect of losing him. They didn't want him to go. They wanted to hold onto him.

But in this they were thinking, not of him, but of themselves. He told them so. He said, 'If you loved me you would have been glad to know that I am going to the Father, for the Father is greater than I.' (John 14:28) To go back to the Father was for Jesus the very goal of his life. To try to hold him back from this was not to show love for him.

Possessive love is very common. Some parents are very possessive in their love for their children. Having given life to them, they refuse to let them live that life in their own way. The same thing happens in some marriages. There is a reluctance to let one's partner have a life of his or her own.

Possessive love causes a lot of pain and does a lot of harm. Non-possesive love, on the other hand, does wonders for both parties.

The Bird Cage

One day a young boy found a shivering little fledgeling lying on the ground, having fallen from its nest. Feeling sorry for it, he took it in-

side and put it by the fire, where it soon revived. The boy was delighted. However, instead of taking it back to its nest, he built a cage
for it. In the cage he gave it all the food, drink, warmth, and care it
could possibly need or desire.

The little bird thrived. Pretty soon its wings grew strong, and it
began to fly around the cage. Next it began to sing. At this the boy
was absolutely thrilled. But one day he noticed that it was beating its
wings violently against the sides of the cage. Unable to figure out
why the bird was doing this, the boy asked his grandfather about it.

'It's not happy,' his grandfather replied.

'I don't understand,' answered the boy. 'Hasn't it got everything
it needs in the cage?'

'Everything except the one thing every bird longs for.'

'What's that?' asked the boy.

'Freedom,' came the reply.

'You mean, after all I've done for it, it wants to leave me?'

'It just wants to be free, so that it can be a bird like other birds.'

'But how can I let it go?' the boy persisted. 'It knows nothing
about the dangers that lie in wait for little birds out in the world. It
might get killed or starve to death.'

'That's a risk you'll have to take.'

'But I love it too much to let it go.'

'If you really loved it, you would let it go.'

The little boy grew silent. He looked at the bird. It continued to
beat its wings against the cage. With every beat it seemed to be saying, 'Set me free! Set me free!'

However, instead of setting it free, the boy built a bigger cage for
it. But soon it was beating its wings against the sides of the bigger
cage too. Then one day it stopped doing so. But on the same day it
stopped singing too.

This situation went on for some time. The bird was unhappy. So
too was the boy. The thing that really got to the boy was the bird's
silence. That silence seemed to grow deeper with each day that

passed. Eventually, unable to endure it any longer, he decided to let the bird go.

As it flew out the window and vanished into the branches of a nearby tree, it took a piece of his heart with it. Feeling lonely and empty, he stared at the open window for a long time. Then all of a sudden he heard the bird's singing coming from the tree. That singing seemed more joyous and melodious than ever before. In an instant the boy felt the wound in his heart heal up and for the first time in months he felt free, happy, and at peace.

'Where there is love there is pain.' Catherine de Hueck Doherty

'In friendship properly and maturely understood, one seeks nothing at all for oneself.' Michel Quoist

'If you love something, set it free. If it comes back to you, it is yours. If it doesn't, it never was.' Anon.

In the Garden

They came to a small estate called Gethsemane, and Jesus said to his disciples, 'Stay here while I go over there to pray.' He took Peter and the two sons of Zebedee with him. And sadness came over him, and great distress. Then he said to them, 'My soul is sorrowful to the point of death wait here and keep awake with me.' And going on a little further he fell on his face and prayed, 'My Father,' he said, 'if it is possible, let this cup pass me by. Nevertheless, let it be as you, not I, would have it.' (Matthew 26:36-39)

Cry for Help

Once I was doing some work close to the Bog of Allen in County Kildare. The sight of such a vast expanse of peatland, as well as the presence of gigantic peat-harvesting machines, tempted me to go for a walk into the bog itself.

It was a dry, windy October afternoon. The surface was suprisingly firm under my feet. When I set off into the bog I didn't stop to consider where exactly I would go. I just headed off into the track of bogland that lay directly ahead of me.

I had gone about half a mile when over to my left I saw a worker's hut. For some strange reason I was attracted to it and wanted to see what it was like inside. I had just reached it when all of a sudden I heard the bleat of a sheep.

'What in heaven's name is a sheep doing in this wilderness?' I asked myself.

I looked around but failed to see the sheep. Then I heard the bleat again. It was coming from a spot directly behind the hut. On making my way around to the back of the hut I saw a ditch which was about ten feet deep. Dark, muddy, water lay at the bottom of it. And there knee deep in the mud, was a sheep. It had obviously slipped into the ditch and was unable to get back out.

The plight of that sheep, especially its feeble heart-rending bleat, went straight to my heart. Even though I could see that it would be a messy business to extricate it, I knew I could not leave it there to die. And die it surely would unless I saved it. It was extremely unlikely that the men who occasionally passed that way on tractors or motorbikes would hear its cry above the noise of their machines.

It took me a while to figure out how best to get it out. The one thing I had to guard against was ending up in the hole myself. Inside the hut I found a spade. With the spade I was able to cut out steps in the bank of peat, and thus I made my way down the side of the ditch. They say sheep are dumb. I swear that this sheep (it was a ewe) came towards me and offered me her head. I grasped her by a horn and took hold of the wool on her back, and slowly, a step at a time, took her out of the hole.

Once I had her out and away from the edge of the pit, I released her. I was glad to see that she was able to stand up. In fact she immediately began to eat the coarse grass that was growing on the bank.

As I made my way home I was no longer thinking of the trouble the sheep had caused me, but only of the joy I felt at having saved a life. But the thing that was most vivid in my mind was the cry of the sheep. And I thought to myself: without that cry, there would have been no happy ending, because I would never have known of its plight.

It isn't only sheep that fall into holes. People fall into them too. But they aren't as smart as sheep, because often they are ashamed to ask, much less to cry for help.

Not so Jesus. He was not ashamed to let his friends see his fear and his distress. Nor was he ashamed to ask for help – their help and that of his heavenly Father.

Someone to Be there with Us

One of the great things in such circumstances is to have someone there beside us. We know that person can't suffer in our place. Still, just to have someone there, someone who understands what we are going through, and who cares about us, is a source of immense comfort and strength. It breathes new life into us like a wind breathes life into a dying fire. Woe to the one who has to face the 'dark valley' alone.

On a Sunday evening in November I was walking by myself in the Dublin mountains. It was beginning to grow dark as I came over the brow of a hill. Before me lay the glittering lights of the city. I feasted my eyes on them. It is comforting to see light ahead when darkness is closing in and you are far from home.

Then I turned around and looked back. Behind me lay a deep valley which was filling up with an awesome darkness. I said to myself, 'What if I had to go back down into that dark valley?' The very thought sent a shudder down my spine. And yet, I thought, I wouldn't hesitate for a second to descend into that valley, if only I had a friendly hand in mine.

Just then the oft-repeated words of Psalm 23 sprang to mind: 'Even if I should walk through the valley of darkness, I would fear no evil, for you are there with your crook and your staff; with these you give me comfort.'

Lord, I hope you'll forgive me, but when I said 'friend', I was thinking of a human friend.

'I need friends in whose friendship I can rest as in a garden.'
Antoine de Saint Exupery

'When someone is at the end of his strength, lend him the support of yours, and see what wonders that can work.' Irina Ratushinkaya

Found Wanting

Unfortunately Jesus' three friends let him down. When he came back to them he found them asleep. It was a poor show on their part, to put it mildly. It wasn't that they didn't know what he was going through. They did. Besides he had specifically asked for their support.

How many times he had come to their aid in their moments of need. And the one time he asked them for help they failed him miserably. He was disappointed in them, especially in Peter. And he let him know this. He said, 'So you do not have the strength to keep awake with me one hour?' (Matthew 26:40)

It's not neccessary that we fall asleep beside the one who is suffering and needs our support. Lack of sensitivity, lack of awareness, and especially indifference, will produce the same effect.

Do You Love Me?

Joe and Mary seemed to have a good marriage. On the tenth anniversary of their wedding, they went out for a meal. Afterwards they retired to a pub for some drinks. They talked for a while over the drinks, then lapsed into silence.

Mary eventually broke the silence. With a note of anxiety in her voice, she turned to Joe and said, 'Joe, do you love me?' And Joe replied at once, 'Yes, I do.' They lapsed into silence again. Joe nodded to the barman who promptly refilled their glasses.

A second time Mary broke the silence. Again she turned to Joe, and with increased anxiety in her voice, asked, 'Joe, do you really love me?' And again without a moment's hesitation Joe replied, 'Yes, Mary, I really do.' They lapsed into silence once more. Again Joe saw to it that their glasses were refilled.

A third time Mary broke the silence. She turned to Joe, and with a quiet desperation in her voice, asked, 'Joe, do you really and truly love me?' On hearing her ask him the same question a third time, Joe got annoyed and answered, 'Mary, how many times do I have to tell you that I love you? Didn't you hear me the first time? Are you drunk or something? However, let me repeat it once again. I really and truly do love you.'

With that Mary shook her head sadly and replied, 'Joe, you don't really love me.' He looked at her with a blank expression on his face. Then mumbled, 'I don't understand.' She looked at him steadily, then said, 'Joe, if you really loved me, you'd know what's hurting me.'

'Love will always find a way, indifference will always find an excuse.' Anon.

'We know too well the sick, sick dread lest the one we love might secretly be indifferent to us.' Walt Whitman

Going on in spite of Everything

Jesus' distress increased to the point where his sweat fell to the ground like drops of blood. He said the same prayer a second and a third time. Then he came back to the three apostles and said, 'Now the hour has come for the Son of Man to be betrayed into the hands of sinners. Get up! Let us go, my betrayer is close at hand.' (Matthew 26:46)

So eventually he found the strength to face what had to be faced. Courage is not never being afraid. It is being afraid, and overcoming it, or continuing on in spite of it.

Where did this extra strength come from? From inside himself. But it took prayer and the support of his friends (such as it was) to make this energy available to him. It seems that there are energies which are not available to us in normal times, but which become available on missions of life and death. These energies are far greater than we think.

So when we say, 'This is the end! I can't take any more!' all it means is that we've come to what our experience believes to be the end of our strength. If we try to forget about tiredness and go on, we will discover that there is no such end inside us. The only end is the end forced on us from outside.

In his wonderful book, *Lost World of the Kalahari,* Laurens van der Post says:

Often in my life I have found that the one thing that can save is the thing which appears most to threaten. In peace and war I have found that frequently, naked and unashamed, one has to go down into what one most fears and in the process, from somewhere beyond all concious expectation, comes a saving flicker of light and energy that even if it does not produce the courage of a hero at any rate enables a trembling mortal to take one step further. (p. 171)

'A heroine is one who sees the danger and is afraid of it, but defies it.' Karen Blixen

'Courage is fear that has said its prayers.' Anon.

'Strange things happen when you have nothing to rely on except God's help.' Irina Ratushinkaya

'Every human being possesses a reserve of strength the extent of which is unknown to him: it can be large, small, or non-existent, and *only extreme adversity makes it possible to evaluate it.'* Primo Levi

Our Greatest Source of Strength

Our spirit is our most precious possession, It is our greatest source of energy. It is to us what wings are to a bird, or roots are to a tree. However, while it is capable of ascending the heights, it is also capable of plumbing the depths.

It can be an oak unmoved in a storm or a frail reed swaying in the wind.

It can be a blazing fire or a dying ember.

It can be a restless stream or a stagnant pond.

It can be a sail filled with wind or a limp flag.

It can be a desert shrub or a hothouse flower.

It can be a piece of granite or a piece of china.

What is it that causes the spirit to sink, and what is that helps it to soar?

Sadness weighs it down; joy lifts it up.

Criticism erodes it; praise builds it up.

Failure shrinks it; success expands it.

Despair causes it to wilt; hope breathes new life into it.

Rejection wounds it; acceptance heals it.

Hatred poisons it; love purifies it.

Fear cripples it; solitude calms it; prayer strengths it.

Hitting Rock Bottom
Luke 22:59-62

On hearing the cock crow, Jesus turned and looked at Peter. Peter looked at him. Their eyes met. Then Peter looked down. He remembered the brave words he had said earlier that evening about being ready to go to prison and even to die for Jesus. How hollow they sounded now. At the time, Jesus had tried to tell him that he didn't know what he was saying, but Peter didn't believe him. He thought he knew better than Jesus. But the crowing of the cock proved who knew best.

What a rich, effective, though painful encounter it was for Peter. Yet during it not a word was said. Where there is love and trust, words are not always necessary. The look of Jesus said it all. It is obvious that it was not a look of condemnation or rejection, but one of understanding and compassion.

'A person's character reveals itself to me at the moment I'm groping for the outline of his face. The most striking thing is to discover the weakness hidden in everyone, the flaw that makes every man touching. You are overcome with compassion when you find in each man the source of tears.' Pablo Picasso

Jesus already knew the flaw in Peter. It was Peter who had to discover it in himself. When he did, he went out and wept bitterly. Oh, the relief of tears, the cleansing power of them, when they come not just from the eyes but also from the heart. Happy those who can shed genuine tears for their sins. They will find not just forgiveness, but also comfort and peace. Pity those who remain dry-eyed – denying, excusing, blaming others. They will remain in their guilt, without consolation.

In wartime, a soldier can be caught too far out of position. An inexperienced swimmer can be caught in currents he can't cope with. Something similar happened to Peter that night. He went beyond his strength, beyond his resources. The knowledge that there is such a position should keep us humble.

This, without doubt, was Peter's lowest moment. That night he hit rock bottom. What saved him from despair was his encounter with Jesus. In it he felt that, not only did Jesus not judge him or write him off, but he actually went on believing in him and loving him.

This is what turned a painful and humbling experience into an hour of grace and salvation. Far from being the end (as it was for Judas), it gave him a chance to make a new beginning. This time he would begin in earnest by building on rock.

In order to build upwards, construction workers begin by going down until they meet rock. When they encounter the rock, then they begin to build. Alexander Solzhenitsyn says:

> When I found myself in the labour camps, I found myself sinking down to the bottom, and felt it firm beneath my feet – the hard, rock bottom that is the same for all. It was the beginning of the most important years in my life. (*Gulag Archipelago*, Vol. 3, p. 98)

> *'Tears flow when words are of no avail.'* Kahlil Gibran

> *'By grief alone is love perfected.'* Anon.

I Do Not Know This Man

On September 27, 1941, in a town in Lithuania, some three thousand Jews were taken from their homes by the SS to the local cemetery. There they were stripped, and shot on the edge of a previously dug pit.

Samuel, a sixteen year-old boy, fell into the pit unharmed, a split second before the bullets killed those near him. When night fell, he climbed out, and still naked, ran to the nearby house of a farmer. But when the farmer saw him he shouted, 'Go back to the grave, Jew, where you belong.' With that he slammed the door in his face. It was the same story at several other doors.

Finally he went to the home of an old widow he knew who lived near the forest. In utter despair, he cried out, 'I am the Lord, Jesus Christ, who has come down from the cross.' Crossing herself, she took him inside, washed, fed and sheltered him. Three days later he joined the partisans in the forest and survived the war.

The Second Calling of Peter

There are two calls of Peter related in the Gospels. The first is rather brief and informal. It occurred by the sea of Galilee at the start of Jesus' ministry. On hearing the call, he dropped everything and followed Jesus (Mark 1:16-18). The second call is more solemn and definitive. It occurred after the resurrection and at the same location. (John 21:1-19)

Three years separated those two calls. During that time a lot of things had happened for Peter. He had found out a lot about the man who called him, the task to which he called him, and above all about himself. When the second call came, Peter was a wiser and humbler man. Therefore, the 'yes' he pronounced this time was far more mature and enlightened.

It is interesting to see that Jesus did not write Peter off because he hadn't come up to scratch. He still believed in him. We all need someone to believe in us, someone who doesn't write us off because we don't come up with the goods at once. It is also interesting to see that Peter did not write off himself.

A vocation is not something one hears once and answers once. The call has to be heard many times, and responded to many times. Each day a part of the chosen path opens up before us, a part we have not trodden before. We have to say 'yes' to the new as we have said 'yes' to the old. As one goes on, the call gets deeper, and the response becomes more interior and more personal.

All vocations are vocations to love – love for the Lord, and love for the sheep and lambs of his flock.

The Fire-maker

The fire-maker was making his way home through the empty streets. Snow was falling, and a bitter wind was blowing. It was no night to hang about out-of-doors. He shivered as he quickened his steps.

He was taking a shortcut across a piece of waste ground when he saw the fire. In truth it was hardly a fire at all – just a bunch of smouldering logs. There was more smoke than fire. Around it, huddled together, was a group of people, their threadbare rags pulled closely around them in the vain hope of warding off the biting cold.

He stopped, not because he really wanted to, but because something inside him would not let him pass. But he made his stay as brief as possible. He made a half-hearted effort to breathe some life into the fire. He felt uneasy in the company of these people. So, having said a few inspirational words about the value of fire to the dark, silent figures, he slunk away.

Yet he had no sooner left them than he felt bad. He thought how he might have kindled that fire if only he had been willing to take the time and the trouble. He could have warmed those pathetic figures with bright flames. But then, what if he had caught pneumonia in the process? And most likely they wouldn't appreciate his efforts. They didn't exactly look like people who would fall all over him in their gratitude. Besides, they were probably used to the cold and in any case knew no better.

These thoughts were jostling one another for possession of his mind when a little further on he came upon another group of people sitting under a roof where a blazing fire burned. 'Come in! Come in!' they shouted at him, noticing his famished appearance. He didn't have to be asked twice. They made room for him in the circle around the fire. 'What a warm-hearted bunch of people!' he said to himself.

He steeped himself in the heat of the fire and allowed the warmth of their welcome to wrap itself around him. He dallied longer than he had intended. Finally, tearing himself away with great reluctance he said without conviction, 'I must be off.'

'Thanks for stopping,' they said in a chorus of voices.

Out in the cold once more he said to himself, 'They actually thanked me. It's I who should have thanked them. It's so nice to be among people who appreciate what a good fire is.'

Once home, he went straight to bed. That night he had a dream in which God appeared to him and said, 'I appointed you as a fire-maker, but you have failed me.' God said no more, but he didn't have to. The fire-maker got the message at once.

He woke up and was unable to get back to sleep. As he lay there his mind went back to his early days as a fire-maker. With what enthusiasm and abandon he had given himself to the job. How glad he was to have chosen, or rather, to have been chosen for such a wonderful calling. What a beautiful occupation was his – to bring warmth into the lives of cold people.

But back then he had no idea of the hard sacrifices his calling would demand of him. Nor had he given much thought to how messy firemaking could sometimes be, and how unresponsive and unappreciative people could be. But over the years all these things were brought home to him. The result was that the spark of his initial enthusiasm gradually died out. The fire of his love grew dim. He grew cold in his vocation.

But on this dark wretched night in which he plumbed the depths of his weakness, this night in which his selfishness had been so cruelly exposed, this night in which his own need for warmth and closeness had been painfully revealed to him, the spark of his vocation was kindled once more in his heart. He made up his mind that next day he would become a fire-maker all over again.

Loved to the End

During the last supper Jesus looked around at the twelve apostles. He had chosen each of them personally, chosen them because he saw good in them. Over a period of three years he had shared everything with them. Yet now he realised that one of them was a traitor. He was very upset and said, 'One of you is about to betray me.' (Matthew 26:21)

On hearing him say this, they were shocked. What was he saying? A traitor among them! Impossible! Now it was their turn to get upset and they started asking him in turn, 'Not I, Lord, surely?' (Matthew 26:22). Jesus intended this. He was trying to touch the heart of the betrayer in the hope that even at this late hour he might see what he was doing and change his mind.

The apostles then asked Jesus to identify the traitor. No doubt they would have dealt with him on the spot. But Jesus refused to point the finger at Judas in front of the others. He wanted him to know that he knew what he was up to, but he was leaving the door open for him to return.

Later in the garden when a mob came forward to arrest Jesus, who was at the head of that mob? Judas! It was he who identified Jesus in the dark, doing so with a kiss, a sign of love. And how did Jesus react? He might have said, 'Judas, you'll pay for this!' But he said nothing of the sort. Instead he said, 'Judas, are you betraying the Son of Man with a kiss?' (Luke 22:48). Saint Matthew says that Jesus actually addressed him as 'My friend.' (26:50). So, even here, he tried one last time to reach him.

The next and last time we hear of Judas is some time later that night or early next morning. When he learned that Jesus had been condemned to death, he was 'filled with remorse and took the thirty silver pieces back to the chief priests and elders, saying, "I have sinned; I have betrayed innocent blood."' (Matthew 27:3). But he got no sympathy from them. They had merely used him. They said, 'What is this to us? That is your concern.' (Matthew 27:4) With that, he flung the money in the sanctuary, went off, and hanged himself.

In the past, we often spoke as if Judas wasn't really a free agent. We've implied that he was merely acting out a role in a plan God had drawn up, a plan which had to be fulfilled, otherwise Jesus would not have died and we would not have been saved. Judas was a free agent. He did not have to do what he did.

When he realised just what it was that he had done, he was filled with remorse and self-disgust. It was so painful that he could not endure it. And so he took the decision to end it all

Judas is a very puzzling character. No one has ever satisfactorily explained what motivated him to do what he did. But one thing that is clear is the fact that Jesus never rejected him. On the contrary, he loved him to the end.

'We don't understand good so how can we hope or presume to understand evil?' Alan Paton

To Bless the Light or to Curse It
Luke 23:39-43

Let us first consider the thief who repented. Some may think that he got off very lightly. After a life of crime, he makes a quick act of contrition, and goes straight to heaven. 'Today you will be with me in paradise.' Today! At the very least, we would have expected him to do a stretch in purgatory.

Those who think he got off lightly betray a shallow understanding of the whole episode. When you think about it, what he did was a tremendous thing. Hanging there on the cross, he did a quick review of his life. And what did he discover? An extremely unpalatable truth – that he has wasted it. A wasted opportunity is one thing. But a wasted life! When he looked back at his life all he could see was a heap of rubble.

How did he react? Did he start excusing himself and blaming others – his upbringing, his environment, his companions … ? Not a bit of it. He brushed all this aside and said, 'I am responsible. I am guilty. I am getting what I deserve.' What a refreshi!ng attitude. Today it is common to blame someone else. There is a disturbing tendency to take responsibility away from the individual.

To do what he did is never easy. Pride makes us try to salvage something. What made his deed so great was the fact that it was now too late to do anything about it, too late to clear away the rubble and start to build again. To do it in the atmosphere which prevailed on Calvary was greater still, given the jeering of the religious leaders, the mocking of the soldiers, and the abuse of his comrade.

Still, his act of repentance, great and all as it was, would have availed him nothing if there was no one there who could help him. But Christ was there – the friend of sinners, the one who claimed to have power to forgive sin. The thief's clean, humble, honest confession went straight to the heart of Christ. It won for him, not only forgiveness, but heaven itself.

From where did his faith in Christ come? We do not know. How deep was this faith? Again we do not know. The only thing we do know is that it was deep enough to enable Christ to save him.

The good thief gives hope to all who come to the end and have nothing that they can feel good about, nothing that they can be proud of in their lives. Even at the eleventh hour there exists the possibility of improving the form of one's past. A person's life consists of a collection of events, the last of which can change the meaning of the whole.

What of the second thief – the unrepentant one? He is a profoundly disturbing character. Even with death staring him in the face, he didn't show a trace of remorse, not the least knawing of conscience. What was going on in the depths of his dark soul? We can't really tell. We can't get beneath the words he said, words which perhaps did not reflect what he really felt, but which may have been prompted by a desire to show off, or to put a brave face on things and salvage some of his pride.

But how come Christ, who could read the secrets of the heart, was not able to reach him? No one can save the person who doesn't want to be saved – not even Christ. The sun can't shine through murky waters or behind closed curtains. It seems that a person can be hardened beyond repentance, broken beyond repair, lost beyond finding. This raises a very serious question: in wrong-doing, is there a point of no return? On this subject Alexander Solzenitsyn says:

> Evil-doing has a threshold. A human being hesitates and bobs back and forth between good and evil all his life. He slips, falls back, clambers up, repents, things begin to darken again. But just so long as the threshold of evil-doing is not crossed, the possibility of returning remains, and he himself is still within reach of our hope. But when, through the density of evil actions, the result either of their own extreme degree or of the absoluteness of his power, he suddenly crosses that threshold, he has left humanity behind, and without, perhaps, the possibility of return. (*Gulag Archipelago*, Vol. 1, p. 175)

Most of the Nazi leaders, in spite of the terrible crimes they committed, showed no remorse, and at the end of the war sought to elude justice. Indeed, some of them, on escaping to South America, went right on with their evil deeds, lending their expertise in torture to rightwing governments.

Stumbling Block or Stepping Stone

Once two travellers were going through a deep forest when night suddenly descended on them. In a matter of minutes, the narrow, indistinct path which they had been following became invisible. In the darkness terror lurked everywhere. Then, to crown it all, a violent thunderstorm broke over the forest. Terrifying flashes of lightning were followed by peals of thunder which shook the ground under their feet. Torrents of rain poured down on them. The trees swayed dangerously.

The first man looked on the storm as a calamity. Every time there was a flash of lightning, he looked up at the sky and cursed God. The result was that he strayed from the path and got lost in the forest. The second man, however, looked on the storm as a blessing in disguise. Each flash of lightning lit up a little bit of the path ahead of him. By keeping his head down, he succeeded in staying on the path. And so, a step at a time, he made his way out of the forest.

The same misfortune can prove a stumbling block to one person and a stepping stone to another.

'Modern man is adept at finding good reasons for doing the wrong thing.' Laurens van der Post

'It is high time for us to stop our pathetic complaining that our environment has ruined us.' Fyodor Dostoyevsky

'One drowning man can't save another.' Mahatma Gandhi

'Not even the greatest artist can play on broken strings.' Michel Quoist

Too Much, too Late

Once, down by the marsh lived a thrush by the name of Melanie. The marsh was flat, dreary and mournful – a bleak place for a thrush. But the ducks, geese, crows, curlews, snipe, jackdaws and gulls didn't seem to mind. In fact these were completely at home there.

The marsh was filled with noise. The winds swept across its watery wastes with a lonesome sighing and moaning. Night and day the monotonous pounding of the waves could be heard coming up from the ocean. The air was rent with the strident cries of gulls, the coarse honking of geese, the harsh quacking of ducks, and the raucous cawing of crows. Yet for all the noise, it was a world devoid of music.

But Melanie's sweet voice changed all this. And what a beautiful voice she had. Later everybody agreed that nothing as sweet had ever been heard in the marsh. When she wasn't searching for food she spent her time perched on a lone beech tree that grew on a knoll which rose up in the middle of the marsh. Morning and evening her joyful music went out from the tree and floated across the bleak marsh.

She never missed a sunrise or a sunset. She sang not because her life was easy or because she wished to show off. She sang simply because she felt that the marsh could do with a little music. She sang even when she didn't feel like singing. On these occasions especially she longed for a little appreciation, but she got none.

The gulls treated her with supreme indifference. They flew past her as if she didn't exist. The jackdaws were jealous of her. Sometimes they would start up a chorus of twittering that made her task almost impossible. The ducks and geese smiled condescendingly on her, and generally regarded her as an object of curiosity. The crows, who always occupied the upper branches of the tree, looked down on her.

Yet behind all these fronts the other birds, almost without exception, secretly admired and appreciated Melanie's singing. Now and then they even admitted as much to one another. But not even a whisper of their admiration reached the ears of Melanie.

Now Melanie was a sensitive little creature. She felt the weight of their disregard. It's hard to sing to an audience that shows no appreciation. Nevertheless, sing she did.

But then one morning the tree was silent. Melanie had died suddenly during the night. The sound of her voice was missed at once. Her body was found on the ground under the beech tree. News of her death spread like lightning across the marsh. Slowly and reverently the other birds gathered around her body. They were overcome with sorrow, and spoke in voices steeped in respect and awe.

'What a pity!' sighed the crows.

'What a shame!' lamented the jackdaws.

'It's too bad!' moaned the ducks.

'It's nothing short of a tragedy!' cried the geese.

'The marsh will not be the same without her!' wailed the gulls.

Many tears were shed and mournful cries drifted over the marsh all that day and late into the night. The birds were inconsolable.

They gave her a funeral such as no bird ever got. They buried her at the foot of the tree which she had adorned for so long with her wonderful singing. Then the jackdaws made a suggestion which met with universal acceptance. As a mark of respect, and as a sign of their undying gratitude to her for all the pleasure she had given them, no one would ever again use the tree. The tree which had provided such a fitting stage for her singing, would remain a silent monument to her memory.

We have an unfortunate habit of keeping our praise under lock and key until the person for whom it is intended has passed away. Then it all rushes out like water from a dam that has suddenly burst its banks.

The Roman centurion who was in charge on Calvary at the crucifiction of Jesus paid a wonderful tribute to him. He declared, 'This was a great and good man' (Luke 23:47). But by that time Jesus was already dead.

The Prince

The town of Harmony, far from living up to its name, was a hotbed of bigotry, prejudice, and discrimination. The king was aware of this, and it was believed that it was only a matter of time before he would take stern action to clean up the mess. Finally he did take action. But no one could have foreseen the extraordinary nature of the action he took.

The Prince came in disguise, unannounced, and without fuss. He moved all over the town. He recognised no barriers. He penetrated into the heart of every ghetto. Everywhere he went, people took to him at once. Rich and poor alike saw something special in him. They sensed that he not only accepted them but also loved them.

The result was that they loved him in return and would do anything to please him.

Time passed. The seeds which he had sown so generously had thrived. He reckoned that the time had come to reap the harvest. He put a lot of thought into how best to do this. Eventually he hit upon a plan. He invited all his friends to come to a level place on a certain day for a great picnic.

A vast multitude turned up. They came from every corner of the town. Every social class, every shade of political opinion, every religious and ethnic group was represented. All were delighted to see the large following their hero had. The sun beamed down on them. So too did the Prince. In a brief speech of welcome he said:

'I'm delighted to see so many of you here today. During the past few months I have been all over town. I have seen the many differences that exist among you. But I'm confident that we can overcome these because I know that there is also a vast untapped reservoir of goodwill among you. I propose that today we begin to tap this reservoir. I would like you, therefore, to mix freely with one another and to share the food and drink you brought. So please sit down and let the picnic begin.'

Up to this point the mood of the crowd had been excellent. But while the Prince was talking the people had an opportunity to look around them and take stock of one another. Suddenly the mood began to change. They were thinking, 'What a strange mixture of people our hero has assembled.' Pretty soon these thoughts found voices.

Looking at the poor, the rich said, 'He sure keeps some strange company!' And the poor, looking at the rich, said, 'How could he mix with snobs like them?' The whites looked at the blacks and said, 'Surely he didn't invite them?' The blacks looked at the whites and said, 'What are they doing here?' And so it went on for the other groups.

The outcome of all this was that they did not mingle with one another as the Prince had asked. Instead they broke into factions. Rather than one large island of people, you had several little islands. Here you had an island of the rich; there an island of the poor. Here one of whites; there one of blacks. Here one of natives; there one of foreigners. Here one of Catholics; there one of Protestants. A cold current flowed in and out between the islands.

Seeing this the Prince was greatly saddened. He went around among them, urging, pleading, begging them to mix with one another. Here and there little groups obeyed him, but these were jeered by the others. As for the vast majority, instead of doing what the Prince had asked, they started to make preparations to leave.

'You tricked us,' some said bitterly. 'You never told us it would be like this.'

'We thought you were on our side,' others said.

Still others said, 'What are you trying to do? Stir up trouble? Isn't there enough trouble in this town already?'

He tried to reason with them. 'Just listen a moment,' he said. 'I assure you that I didn't bring you here to divide you or to set you against one another. I brought you here to unite you.'

'Go away!' they shouted back, and a few clods of earth flew through the air. He struggled on, 'I only wanted to highlight how much we have in common.'

'You're talking nonsense!' they roared in a chorus. 'We have nothing in common.' Now stones began to fly through the air. One stuck the Prince on the shoulder. He tried to continue but they drowned him out.

'Leave us alone!' they shouted. 'Go back to where you came from!'

They drove him away. Their shouts and screams of hatred filled the air. The hail of clods and stones darkened the sky. Covered in blood and abuse, the Prince cut a sorry figure as he departed. The few voices that were raised in his defence died like a whisper in a storm.

At the very moment the Prince disappeared over the horizon a loud clap of thunder was heard. Then the sky opened and rain began to pour down on them. They looked in desperation for cover. Without a moment's hesitation, the whole multitude of people ran in panic towards the one source of shelter in the vast open plane – an old temple which stood a few hundred yards away. They all reached it safely. Though the temple had stout, circular walls it was open to the sky, so they got drenched to the skin.

As they stood there, huddled together like a flock of sheep gathered into a pen, they saw streaks of lightning blazing down towards them from a threatening sky. They were petrified with fear. They knew they had done a terrible thing to their beloved Prince. Obviously God was punishing them.

In their panic they had forgotten their differences. Here they were, packed tightly together in all sorts of combinations. And they felt not the slightest hostility towards one another. The circular walls of the temple had the effect of binding them together as members of one large family. Fear had succeeded where love had failed.

Eventually the storm passed. As they emerged from the temple, the sun shone down warmly on them once more. In an instant it dried their wet clothes. And suddenly they realised that something wonderful had happened. All their fear of, and hatred for, one another had evaporated. Then they realised that, far from punishing them as they deserved, God had taken pity on them and cleansed them.

In the twinkling of an eye all barriers fell down and they embraced one another. Then they sat down and the real picnic began. It went on with much merriment until sundown. It was only on the way home that it began to dawn on them what the Prince had done for them. He had brought the boil of their sectarianism to a head. Then he had lanced it. The poison flowed all over him and he had borne it away on his body.

Later when they discovered his true identity, they were overwhelmed. Their love for him overflowed. They dearly longed to be able to make amends to him, but saw that this was not possible. So they did the next best thing – they made amends to one another for the way they had hitherto treated one another. They realised that this was the reason the king had sent the Prince among them.

And from that day onwards the town of Harmony began to live up to its name.

Wounded by Doubt

Before and after

In what follows we imagine Thomas talking about his experience of losing faith and regaining it.

Before, I was walking along a broad and straight road towards a sure and exciting destination. I had a leader to guide me, and friends to accompany me. The sun was shining warmly on us as we travelled light-heartedly along. Afterwards, the sun refused to give its light. My guide was struck down. My friends vanished. I was alone on the road, except that it was no longer a road, but a narrow, winding path leading I knew not where.

Before, I was like a sunflower which during the day turns its head so that it is always facing the sun. But when the sun goes down, and the world grows dark, it closes its petals and hangs its head. When the sun went down on the Master's life I wilted. Without him my days lacked all charm and life became a desert.

Before, I felt like an oak, sturdy and solid. Now I was like a reed shaking in the winds of doubt. The truth, of course, was, though I didn't realise it at the time, that it was the Master who was the oak. I was a mere sapling growing in his shade. When the oak fell I was defenceless.

All of this was partly my own fault. When I think back I can see that my following of him was almost totally blind. I was enthusiastic and generous, but unreflective. Yet I knew he didn't want blind followers. Quite the opposite. He tried to open people's eyes. He didn't threaten or coerce. He invited. He wanted people to follow him freely, and with both eyes open. Above all, he wanted people to follow him with the heart.

I made things even more difficult for myself by cutting myself off from the others. When they claimed that they had seen him, I could see a difference in them. Their darkness had lifted. Joy and peace radiated from them. Their fear was gone. They began to move out. There was a spring in their step. It was clear that someone had breathed new life into them.

But I was still in the dark, still excluded from the banquet of joy and peace. I refused to take their word for it. I had to be sure. Having been let down once, I was determined it wouldn't happen a second time. But I was stubborn too. I was like a person who curses the darkness, yet when someone tells him that the day has dawned, still refuses to pull back the curtains.

Why, you may ask, did I have to touch him? Wasn't seeing him enough? I had to touch him in order to be healed. I'd seen others healed by touching him. Some of these were healed by touching just the hem of his robe, so strong was their faith. But my faith was so weak that I had to touch him, and not just his hands but his side as well.

In truth, I was the wounded one. I was wounded by unbelief and despair. My heart was broken with grief. My mind darkened by doubt. Even though these wounds were invisible, they were nevertheless absolutely real. But he was able to see them. It was he who touched my wounds, and so made me whole and well again.

'The human heart is healed only by the presence of another human being who understands human pain.' Anon.

Sunday Morning Stream

To be a believer or just a spiritual person in today's world can often be a lonely business. Here is where the community comes in. It is only with the help of the community that we can resolve our doubts and sustain our faith.

It was a sunny Sunday morning in early April. The snowdrops had handed over the torch of spring to the primroses. On my way into Dublin I passed through a small town. Trickles of people were filtering from every street and forming into little pools. Soon the pools joined up to form streams. Near the church the streams became a river.

They came in ones, twos, and larger groups. Every age-group was respresented. It was a heartening sight. God's scattered children were being gathered together. God's fragmented family was being reunited.

But then I asked myself: How many of these people realise the greatness of what they are doing? How many of them are really free, and not prisoners of routine or supersition? How many are mere driftwood being carried along by the stream? If there was no current flowing, or if it was flowing in the opposite direction, how many of them would be here?

Suddenly, however, the power of example came home to me, and I saw the whole thing in a more positive light. We create a current that makes it easier for one another to go to the Father's house.

This week I may be feeling weak and apathetic. Therefore I unashamedly yield myself to the current and allow myself to be carried. Next week, who knows? I may be feeling strong and enthusiastic, and so I will help carry someone else.

'Surely God will understand my doubts in a world like this?' Etty Hillesum, who died in Auschwitz

'It is harder to believe than not to believe.' Flannery O'Connor

'I am not religious, but I respect the believer and sometimes envy him.' Primo Levi

'Doubt is as necessary to faith as air is to fire.' Elie Wiesel

What Is Essential Is Invisible

'Unless I see, unless I touch, I will not believe' – so said Thomas. It sounds very reasonable and very logical. It represents the rational approach so much in vogue today. Today the opinion prevails that everything can be rationally explained. If something is obscure, all we have to do is shed a ray of scientific light on it and it will become clear.

Of course we must be guided by reason, but we also have to listen to the imagination and the heart. There are aspects of life which cannot be rendered by purely rational means. Science isn't everything.

To adopt Thomas' approach would be to condemn ourselves to living in a material world. But some of the most important ingredients of life can neither be seen nor touched. There is a layer of reality which eludes the senses but which, nevertheless, is absolutely real. The visible world is only part of a greater world which includes invisible realities from which it draws its chief significance. As the Little Prince said, 'What is essential is invisible.'

Seeing and hearing can be crutches which prevent us from thinking, feeling, and imagining. Often the handicapped have more feeling and more perception than the so-called normal. Vision, insight, understanding, perception, have little to do with seeing. Many people prefer facts to vision.

Nevertheless, we can sympathise with Thomas. He was merely echoing the human cry for certainty. However, here on earth there is no absolute certainty about God and spiritual realities. We have to be content with 'seeing a dim reflection in a mirror'. We are not so much looking through an open door as peering through a chink. This chink is big enough to let the light in but not so big as to eliminate wonder and mystery.

'*Behind all seen things lies something vaster; everything is but a path, a portal, or window opening on something other than itself.*' Antoine de Saint Exupery

'*Pity the eye that sees no more in the sun than a stove to heat it and a torch that lights its way between home and office.*' Kahlil Gibran

'*It is necessary sometimes to believe in something a little in order to see it.*' Vincent Van Gogh

'*The most beautiful experience we can have is the mysterious.*' Albert Einstein

Witnessing with Wounds

Primo Levi, the Italian writer, at a distance of forty years, still bore the tatoo he got in Auschwitz. He said:

> I don't glory in it, nor am I ashamed of it, I do not display it, and do not hide it. I show it unwillingly to those who ask out of pure curiosity; readily, and with anger, to those who say they are incredulous. Often young people ask me why I don't have it erased, and this surprises me: why should I? There are not many of us in the world to bear witness. (*The Drowned and the Saved*, p. 95)

Alexander Solzhenitsyn says that he still has the four patches bearing the number he was given in the prison camps. He was not the only one to have brought them out of the camps. He says, 'In some houses they will be shown to you like holy relics.'

It's interesting that Jesus kept the marks of the nails and the spear on his risen body. One might have expected him to have shed them to show that all that was behind him, or so as not to embarrass the apostles who abandoned him, and the people who were directly or indirectly responsible for causing them.

For Jesus those wounds were not things to be ashamed of or embarrassed about. They were the living proof of his love, the tangible and telling signs of how costly real love can be. They were more like badges of honour, or hard-won medals of distinction. They were still wounds but the poison had gone out of them, and so they no longer hurt.

It is comforting for us to learn that Jesus kept the wounds on his risen body. Because they are still visible they have become a source of hope for all of us, especially for those who have suffered and who still suffer.

So many times we want to hide our wounds. We want to cover up the hurts of the past. Even when they have healed outwardly, often the poison remains, so that they still hurt. If we love, we must be prepared to get wounded. However, it would serve no great purpose if we thereby were poisoned by bitterness and resentment.

The Sting

Ellen was in high spirits when she set out to deliver flowers to her friend Mary. She was singing as she went along when, out of the blue, a wasp swooped and stung her in the arm. What had been a sweet journey suddenly turned sour.

Leaving aside the flowers, she sat down by the side of the road to inspect the damage. She had no difficulty in locating the spot in which she had been stung for it felt very sore, had turned red, and was swelling up alarmingly. As she sat there wincing with pain and feeling very sorry for herself, a passerby came to her aid.

'I know exactly how you feel. I've often been stung myself,' said the passerby.

'But why did the wasp have to pick on me? I did nothing to provoke him,' said Ellen.

The stranger made no reply. Instead she took out a jar of ointment and applied some of it to the wound. The ointment had a soothing effect on the wound, and soon Ellen was on her way again. However, as she went along, she couldn't keep her eyes off the wound. Fortunately the swelling subsided and the pain eased up.

Along the way she met up with other travellers. She insisted on telling them about the wasp sting and even showing them the wound. With every telling, the wasp got more vicious and the wound more serious. Though her confidants could barely make out the wound, they could see that Ellen was very bitter about it. All of them tried to help her.

'Ignore the whole thing,' said one.

'Bury it,' said a second.

'Treat it as if it never happened,' said a third.

And so it went on. Though her advisers used different expressions, their advice came to the same thing – forget the sting. This sounded like good advice and she grasped at it.

She tried to forget the sting. God knows she tried. However, memory is a strange thing. We forget the things we want to remember, and we remember the things we want to forget. So, no matter how hard she tried, she could not forget. The sting just would not stay forgotten. It kept up like a decapitated weed. And every time it popped up she felt a stab of pain.

This might have gone on forever had she not had the good fortune to meet up with an old and wise friend by the name of Sheila. Naturally she opened her heart to her also.

'Forget the whole thing! Why should you forget it?' asked Sheila.

The question surprised Ellen. She hesitated, then replied, 'Everybody I meet tells me that I must forget it.'

'But it happened,' Sheila insisted gently. 'It's part of the story of your journey. Besides, it's not something to be ashamed of.'

'But the thing is that every time I remember it, I feel the hurt all over again,' said Ellen.

'It's how you remember it that matters,' said Sheila. 'You're on a mission of love, aren't you?'

'Yes.'

'Well then, don't let the sting distract you from that. Above all, don't let its poison diminish your love. Then when you arrive at your friend's house, your gift will be all the more precious because you suffered a wound in delivering it.'

After they parted, Ellen reflected on what her friend had said. Then she began to see the sting in a new light. With that the bitterness gradually left her, and once again she found herslf going along with a happy step.

'People can live through great hardships yet perish from hard feelings.' Alexander Solzhenitsyn

'Bitterness is the worst of all evil – it is internal decay.' Elie Wiesel

'Of all wounds, self-inflicted ones go deepest. They are the most difficult to heal, the hardest to forgive, and their scars are impossible to conceal.' Carl Jung

The Wings of Faith

In some ways faith is like flying. You leave the world of the firm and the familiar, yield yourself to invisible currents, and set forth for a destination you cannot see.

At times you are flying in an ocean of light and space. There isn't a cloud in sight. Above you lies the infinity of space. Below you the grandeur of the green earth and blue sea. Though you are suspended between heaven and earth, you feel in touch with both. Above and below are joined together, giving the sense that the world is one and belongs entirely to you. In such moments you get a wonderful feeling of unity and freedom. It's not so lonely then. You feel part of a great whole which is filled with beauty and meaning.

But then come the cloudy days in which the unity of the world is broken. At times the clouds are so low that you have to fly above them. This is another experience altogether. You are up there in brilliant sunshine. The earth has vanished. The sky is still visible, but it has an awesome look about it. Below you is a blanket of white clouds like a soft woolly carpet of virgin snow. You are in a strange and alien world. You feel very isolated.

Then there are times when the opposite happens. You are flying below the clouds. Now it is the sky that has vanished. All you see is the earth and the sea. You don't feel so much cut off as hemmed in.

Finally there are times when you have no choice but to fly right through the clouds. This is an eerie and scary experience. Everything familiar has vanished. There are no landmarks or skymarks of any kind. You are enveloped in a swirling fog and a clinging mist. The way forward is opaque. The way back is swallowed by darkness. Every bit of colour has been snuffed out. You are like a solitary prisoner in a windowless cell. You press forward, trusting that sooner or later a break will appear above or below you. This is faith at its purest.

The Storyteller
Luke 24:13-35

'And now,' said the guide, 'we come to the most famous picture in the gallery. It was painted by the Dutch painter, Rembrandt. It shows Jesus sitting at table between two of his disciples. To appreciate it fully, you'd need to know the story behind it. Do you have a little time?'

'Yes,' came the reply from the group.

Among the group were Mr and Mrs Browne who had recently buried their only son who had been killed in a car accident. They were still in a state of shock, and had come to the museum that day only in the hope that it might take their minds off it for a while. As the guide started the story they were only half listening.

'On Easter Sunday evening,' he began, 'two of Jesus' disciples were returning to Emmaus from Jerusalem. Their hearts were heavy with sorrow. The death of Jesus had plunged them into an impenetrable gloom. Their dreams about him being the long-awaited Messiah had been reduced to rubble. As they went along they were talking about his death. They went over it again and again. They looked at it from every possible angle, and still couldn't make the slightest sense of it. At a certain point a stranger caught up with them.

'"What were you talking about?" the stranger asked.

'"About Jesus of Nazareth," they replied.

'"What about him?" he asked.

'The question surprised them, so they said, "Do you mean to tell us that you've come from Jerusalem and you haven't heard about him?"

'"Tell me about him," he insisted gently.

'The two began to tell the stranger about Jesus. They told about the wonderful things he had said, and the extraordinary things he had done. How everyone looked on him as a great prophet – everyone but the religious authorities, who mounted a campaign against him, a campaign which ended with Jesus being executed by the Romans.

'They paused, then added sadly, "He's already three days dead. We were convinced that he was the Messiah. But now we know that we were mistaken. A humiliated, crucified Messiah! It's impossible. It's unthinkable."

'With that they fell silent. The stranger had listened to all this without saying a word. Now it was his turn to speak.

'"Oh, you foolish people!" he exclaimed. "You think that because Jesus died like this he couldn't possibly be the Messiah. Haven't you read what the prophets said about the Messiah?"

'"We have," they answered feebly.

'"Well then, why didn't you believe them?"

'"What do you mean?" they asked.

'"The prophets foretold that the Messiah would suffer and die, and that it would be precisely in this way that he would enter into his glory. How can anyone attain to glory except through sacrifice and suffering?"

'They looked at him, dumbfounded. Then starting with Moses he went through all the prophets, interpreting for them all the passages that referred to the Messiah. In so doing he turned their image of the Messiah upside down. He shed the image of a conquering hero and donned the robe of a suffering servant.

'Before they knew it they reached Emmaus. By now night was falling. The stranger made as if to continue his journey, but they said to him, "It's getting late. Why don't you stay the night with us?" He agreed to do so. Later when they were at table, the stranger took bread, blessed it, broke it, and gave it to them. In that instant their eyes were opened and they recognised that the stranger was Jesus.'

After a brief pause, the guide said, 'Now I'd like you all to look again at the picture.' The eyes of all returned to the picture. Then the guide resumed, 'It is precisely this moment which the artist has tried to capture – the moment when the eyes of the two disciples were opened so that they were able to recognise Jesus.'

The group looked at the picture long and adoringly, expressing amazement at how marvellously the artist had captured the joy of that moment. But eventually they moved off to other parts of the museum, all except the Brownes. Approaching the guide they said, 'We've heard that story umpteen times, but each time it left us untouched – until now. You told it with so much feeling and conviction.'

'There was a time when I told it very badly,' the guide replied.

'What happened to change this?' the Brownes asked.

'Two years ago my wife got cancer, and died a slow, agonising death. I could see absolutely no meaning in her terrible suffering and untimely death. She was a good person. She didn't deserve all this. I was heart-broken. It was as if the world had come to an end. Nevertheless, I was persuaded to go back to work here at the museum. Once again I found myself telling the story, only more mechanically than before.

'Then one day something clicked with me, and suddenly I realised that the story was about me too. Like the two disciples, I was going down a sad and lonely road. Even though I'm a believer, sadly up to this, Jesus had been little more than a shadowy figure who lived only in the musty pages of the Gospels. But now he came alive for me. I felt his presence at my side, the presence of a friend who knew all about human suffering.

'It was as if at that moment my eyes were opened so that I could see things differently. My heart began to burn within me. As I went on telling the story, a healing process was at work inside me. Even though at times I'm still fragile, I have begun to hope and live again.'

By this time the Brownes were unable to hold back their tears. 'Strange,' they said, 'but as you told the story earlier, we too felt our hearts burn within us.' Then they told him the story of the tragic death of their son. They chatted further over a cup of coffee. As they parted the Brownes said,

'Thank you for what you did for us. You are a true storyteller.'

Sharing the Story

Even though we may never have been to the Holy Land, most of us have been on the road to Emmaus, and have experienced the journey of the two disciples in some shape or form. Some people are very familiar with that road. It represents the road of disappointment, failure, sorrow, grief, shattered dreams ... Fortunate are those who have someone with whom they can share the story of their journey.

Jesus invited the two disciples to talk about their problems. With a simple, direct question, asked in a kindly manner, he got them to open up. It can be easier to talk to a sympathetic stranger than to a friend. When they started to talk, he listened, and did not speak again until they had finished.

In dealing with people who are hurting, it is not enough to listen just with the ears. We have to listen with the heart also. We have to listen patiently and lovingly, in such a way that we invite all that is dammed up in the other person to pour out.

By listening with understanding and without judging, we take on ourselves a share of the other person's pain and transgressions, if there are transgressions. Thus we help him to bear the burden of his pain and shame. The knowledge that one is truly being listened to is of itself remarkably therapeutic. The speaker knows he is not speaking into a void. What he says is being received, and received in such a way that it is transformed, alleviated, and redeemed in the process.

Unshared fears and problems, hurts and wounds, acquire a lot of power over us. But when we share them with another person whom we trust, they lose some of this power. We can then gradually begin to put them behind us, and are able to move forward once more.

One is never done with injury until the moment one is able to put it into words and speak it openly to at least one sympathetic and understanding person. Then one can shed the hurt as a snake sheds its dead skin, and one is ready for the future.

The ability to listen well is a very great gift.

'All sorrows can be borne if you tell a story about them.' Karen Blixen

Our Eyes Are Opened – but only later

Life for all of us is a journey. Faith doesn't save us from the dark, lonely, sorrowful stretches of road. Sadly, when we most need it, our faith seems to fail us. When we are plunged into gloom, we find that the lamp of faith has no oil in it.

It was not until it was all over, that the two disciples understood fully what had happened to them on that journey. Only later did they come to realise how near to them was the one they thought was dead and gone.

But isn't this how it always is in real life? When we are going through the experience, we have no perspective, no understanding. We have enough to do just to cope from day to day or hour to hour. It's only afterwards, perhaps long afterwards, that our eyes are opened so that we begin to understand that experience. Hence the importance of reflecting on our experience. Otherwise we may have the experience but miss the meaning of it.

Eventually we may even be grateful for that experience because we are the better for having been through it. And so we begin to understand the message of his death and resurrection – glory attained through suffering. What other way is there to attain to glory?

'Life lies behind us as the quarry from whence we get tiles and cope-stones for the masonry of today.' Ralph Waldo Emerson

The give-away

How do we recognise friends before we can actually see them? There are as many answers to this question as there are friends. Sometimes the 'give-away' is quite trivial, maybe a mere foible or eccentricity – the sound of a footstep, the accent, the way he rings the doorbell. Other times it is something deeper and more substantial. For example, we receive a generous gift. Even before we look at the name of the donor we say to ourselves, 'This can only be from So-and-so'. Nine times out of ten our guess is correct. Here the 'give-away' is a personal quality.

How did the two disciples recognise Jesus? They recognised him when he took the bread, broke it, and began to share it with them. What does this tell us about Jesus?

Making Disciples

One day the Master called six of his disciples and said to them, 'Go out and make disciples.' And the six set off at once. Time passed and, one by one, they returned.

The first came back with five hundred disciples.

'How did you manage to gain so many?' the Master asked.

'I went around among the poorer sections of the people,' the disciple answered. 'There I found great poverty, suffering and want. I promised them that we would take care of all their needs.'

'I see,' said the Master.

The second came back with four hundred disciples.

'And what approach did you use?' the Master asked.

'I told them about heaven and the great reward that is waiting there for the followers of our way,' was the reply.

'I see,' said the Master.

The third came back with three hundred disciples.

'What approach did you use?' the Master asked.

'I pulled no punches,' this disciple replied. 'I told them they would all go to hell unless they followed our way. They were still not entirely convinced until I worked a miracle. I cursed a mad dog and it dropped dead. That convinced them.'

'I see,' said the Master.

The fourth came back with two hundred disciples.

'What approach did you use?' the Master asked.

'I decided to go around among the simple and uneducated. I convinced them with arguments. I blinded them with knowledge.'

'I see,' said the Master.

The fifth came back with one hundred disciples.

'And what approach did you use?' asked the Master.

'I went among the young,' the disciple replied. "I told them about our way. Then I simply commanded them, and this is the result. They were standing around, waiting for a leader. If I hadn't got to them, then some false messiah would have got to them and exploited them.'

'I see,' said the Master.

Finally, after a long delay, the sixth returned with only a dozen disciples.

'What kept you so long?' the Master asked.

'I wasn't able to sow the seed at once,' the reply began. 'There is no point in sowing the seed in the middle of winter. You have to wait for the snow to melt and the ground to soften. So I waited. As I waited I befriended them, trying to give them an example of our way by the kind of life I lived.

'While I was sharing their lives I discovered that freedom was very important to them. To deprive them of this would be to undermine their dignity and greatly to devalue their consent. I also learned something else about them. I learned that they are a very generous people and not afraid of sacrifice. I told them about the cost of discipleship, but I stressed the good they could do for others and for God as disciples. They seemed impressed. However, when the crunch came, only twelve agreed to come with me.'

The Master commended the last disciple.

Reading the Good Book

Christopher was a practising Christian. Never missed church on a Sunday. He and his family lived in a comfortable house in a fashionable part of town. With good health, and a secure, well-paying job, he was happy and satisfied.

However, there was one thing which bothered him. It concerned his next-door neighbour. The man not only never darkened the door of a church but was a professed agnostic. As a Christian, Christopher felt it was his responsibility to try to convert him. But how was he to do it? On a number of occasions, in talking with him, he had brought up the subject of religion, doing so as delicately as he could. Alas, he had got nowhere.

Then one day he had an inspiration. If only he could get his neighbour to read the Gospels, that would surely do the trick. Who could fail to be moved by the Gospels? The only problem was how to get a copy of the Gospels to him. He couldn't very well knock on the man's door and hand him a copy. That was more likely to put him off. He would have to be more subtle in his approach. So what did he do? He posted a copy to him anonymously – an attractively produced and beautifully illustrated edition.

Having done this, he waited to see what would happen. Days went by and nothing happened. There wasn't the slightest indication from next door that the man had seen the light. About two weeks later, Christopher's wife went next door to return something she had borrowed. When she came back she said,

'You know that copy of the Gospels you sent him?'

'Yes.'

'It's in the refuse bin.'

Christopher was not just disappointed. He was indignant. It was not right to throw the Good Book into the refuse bin. He went next door, picking up the copy of the Gospels as he passed the refuse bin.

'I hope you don't mind me intruding,' he said to his neighbour. 'But I found this in your refuse bin. You know, if only you'd read it, you might find God.'

'But I do read it,' came the surprising reply. 'I read it every day.'

'I don't understand,' said Christopher.

'You are a Christian, aren't you?'

'Why, yes.'

'Well, I've been reading your life every day for the past ten years.'

By This All Will Know

At first the little fruit tree felt lost in the midst of the forest. It was surrounded by great trees. The sight of those mighty trees made it feel insignificant. They were so tall, strong, and useful. It was so small, weak, and useless. So what did it do? It set about gaining a place and a standing for itself in the forest.

How hard it worked and how well it succeeded! In time its head reared up into the sky so that it was able to hobnob with the tallest trees of the forest. Its branches spread outwards like a giant umbrella, claiming more and more space for themselves. It's trunk grew stout and strong so that it was able to laugh at the storms which from time to time roared through the forest.

But then one day the man who planted it made an unexpecteded appearance in the forest. Looking at the tree, he said,

'My, how tall you've grown! Why, you have the most wonderful branches I've ever seen. and your trunk is like the outer wall of a castle.'

'But I still have many faults,' said the tree, feigning humility. 'Just look at all the hollows, clefts, and knots. If only I could rid myself of them I'd look a whole lot better. But I'm working on them.'

'Those faults are of no concern to me. In fact, I don't even see them as faults,' the man replied. On hearing this the tree began to glow with pride and self-satisfaction. But then the man added, 'However, there is one thing I'm not happy with.'

'Oh, so you're not happy with me,' the tree responded, suddenly becoming defensive. 'I don't understand. You can see for yourself that I've prospered. I can hold my own with the oaks and elms. I thought you might be proud of me. I've worked so hard to secure the standing I now enjoy amongst the other trees.'

'I don't doubt for one minute that you've worked hard,' said he.

'Well then, what more do you want from me?"

'The one thing I was hoping to find in you is missing,' he replied.

'You've neglected the most important thing of all – the one thing necessary.'

'What's that?' asked the tree disconsolately.

'Fruit,' came the reply. 'You are not a pine or an oak or an elm. You are something far rarer and more precious. You are a fruit tree. I was depending on you to provide wholesome fruit for the many famished little creatures who roam the forest. But you have failed to do so because you have forgotten what you are. You have become just another tree in the forest.'

Look at the Flowers of the Field

Once upon a time a flower-lover by the name of Amadeus took pity on the wild flowers. Having built a large greenhouse, he roamed the fields and hillsides in search of wild flowers. On finding a flower, he carefully dug it up and transplanted it to the greenhouse.

When he had them all gathered in he proceeded to lavish attention on them. How they thrived! The greenhouse was transformed. All the colours of the rainbow were visible in it. All the perfumes of Arabia were let loose in it. Amadeus was highly pleased with himself.

However, one day he noticed to his surprise that even though his charges were thriving, they didn't seem happy.

'What's the matter?' he asked.

'We don't want to sound ungrateful, but we really think that our place is not in here but out in the fields and hillsides,' a violet answered.

'I don't understand,' said Amadeus, deeply disappointed.

'It's like this,' a primrose added. 'We believe that we have a God-given task to perform.'

'A task! What task?'

'Our task is to be witnesses to God's care for creation,' the primrose replied. 'Was it not of us that the Lord was speaking when he said, "Look at the flowers of the field. See how beautiful they are. I tell you not even Solomon in all his glory was robed like one of these"?'

Amadeus thought for a while. Then he said, 'You know, you're absolutely right. I never looked at it like that before.'

And being a true lover of flowers, that very day he restored them to their natural habitat.

There they were once again assailed by a relentless wind, became a prey to every kind of bug, and had to make do with the scanty food they managed to scrounge from a thin soil. Nevertheless, they were happy because their lives glowed with meaning.

'God grows weary of great kingdoms, but never of little flowers.'
Rabindranath Tagore

He Taught Them in Parables

Visitation

By all accounts John was doing well for himself. He had a good job and an enviable lifestyle. But all of a sudden a dark cloud appeared overhead. Martin, his ageing father, was found to have a terminal illness. He was rushed to a city hospital some sixty miles from where John lived. There he spent the last nine months of his life.

Martin had been a good father. He had worked hard to see that his children would have a better life than he had. John was his only son. Naturally you would expect him to visit his dying father. He visited him four times during those last nine months.

The first visit took place on the afternoon of a public holiday in March when a parade was held in the city.

'And how are you feeling, Dad?' John asked.

'Not bad, son, not bad,' the father replied.

'I brought the kids up to see the parade, so I thought I'd pop in to see you while I was here,' John continued.

'And how was the parade?' asked the father.

'Oh, it was really great. One of the largest and most colourful ever. The kids really enjoyed it.' And they talked about the parade for the next half hour.

The second visit took place towards the end of May.

'And what brings you to the city this time?' asked the father.

'There's a seminar on – all about computers. Fascinating stuff! This is the future,' John. answered. And they talked about computers for half an hour.

The third visit took place in early August.

'And what brings you to the city this time?' asked the father.

'There's a horse show on. I want to buy a pony for the kids,' John replied.

'I see,' said the father. And they talked about the show for half an hour.

The fourth visit took place on a Sunday evening in September.

'And what brings you to the city this time?' asked the father, who was obviously going down hill fast.

'I came up to see a football game. And a right good game it was,' John replied.

'I see,' said the father. And they talked about the game for half an hour.

Martin died on the evening of December 7th.

'What a pity he didn't last one more day,' said John to a neighbour who had come to sympathise with him. "I was planning to visit him tomorrow afternoon. The wife and I were going up to the city to do the Christmas shopping.'

Someone To Be There

Frank, a very zealous priest, had been getting by without a housekeeper. However, he got tired of coming home to four walls. In his own words, 'I wanted someone to be there when I came home.' So he placed an advertisement in the papers for a live-in housekeeper, and was lucky to get a very good person by the name of Sheila.

He said he wanted someone to be there. He now had someone. He never said he wanted someone to talk to. Just someone to be there. He never talked to Sheila, if you exclude a few crumbs of conversation at mealtimes. He treated her more or less as a piece of furniture you place in an empty room to take the bare look off things.

Sheila felt this. Prior to this she had been living in a small country town where she had raised a family of nine. Her husband was dead. Though now in her sixties, she felt she still had something to offer.

When she came to Frank's parish in the city, she knew nobody. Frank was out all day. She longed for someone to talk to. She understood that Frank had a lot of calls on his time. Nevertheless, she wished he would sit down and talk to her, at least now and then.

Frank wanted her to be there for him. And she was there – as faithful as a tabernacle lamp. But he seemed oblivious of the fact that lamps need tending if they are to keep on burning – at least the human ones do.

Too Big a Risk

Alexander wanted to write an article about the war, so he decided to go to the front. He wanted to see for himself what it was like for the soldiers on the ground.

At the front he spared himself nothing. Not once but several times he dashed into the thick of battle. He spent his nights making careful notes of all he had seen during the day. After about a month he decided he had seen enough. So he headed back to his office in the city.

It took him the best part of three weeks to complete his article. He showed it to his editor who was highly pleased with it. It was given centre-page prominence and spread over five days. It created a big stir among the readers. Alexander was purring with self-satisfaction.

But then one day out of the blue came a letter. It was from a soldier who had served at the front but who was now hospitalised with a serious leg wound. In his letter the soldier said,

'I know you meant well. Nevertheless, what you did, praiseworthy though it was, does not entitle you to speak on our behalf. There is an unbridgeable gap between the bravest correspondent and the ordinary soldier. As a journalist you were not part of the force. You were not subject to military discipline. No one would charge you with desertion if you ran away.

'If you really and truly want to understand what it is like for us, you would have to join the unit, fight with it, and not know if you will live or die, or if your comrades will live or die.'

Even though he knew the soldier was speaking the truth, Alexander was deeply hurt by the letter. If he really wanted to be an authentic spokesman for the soldiers, there was only one way to do it – become a soldier himself.

The big question was: good and brave man though he was, was he capable of so big a risk?

On a Pedestal

I'm up here on this pedestal, not able to touch or be touched. I admit that in the beginning I liked it. It's nice to be noticed and regarded. It's certainly better than lying in some dark corner, forsaken and forgotten.

But gradually I came to dislike it. It's terrible to feel that you are always on display. People expect you to be perfect. You end up a prisoner of peoples' expectations.

Right now, I hate being up here. I'm obliged to behave in ways that are false. At times I feel like flinging myself from this pedestal. How wonderful it would be to experience even a moment's relief from the necessity of being perfect.

People who admire and praise me don't know me any better than those who despise and criticise me. I have enemies too, you know.

Some of these are just envious of me. They think I'm having a wonderful time up here. Others say that it was I who put myself up here, because I felt superior and wanted to show off.

Being up here makes me vulnerable before my friends and my enemies, because my faults are on display as well as my virtues. Were I to fall off, my friends would be very disappointed. They'd say I let them down. Some of them would never forgive me. Why, they won't tolerate a wobble, not to mind a fall. As for my enemies, how they would rejoice to see me fall. The greater the fall, the happier they would be.

I'm sick of it all. I just wish people would allow me to be myself.

How Not to Imitate the Saints

Once there was a young man by the name of Simon who, wishing to live a holy life, decided to model himself on Francis of Assisi. He was deadly serious about it. He had only one goal in life – to turn himself into a copy of Saint Francis.

Years went by. There was no doubt that outwardly at least he had made progress. His friends jokingly said he had become a Saint Francis look-alike. Yet he was not happy. In his unhappiness he went to consult a wise old monk by the name of Barnabas. Barnabas listened patiently as Simon poured out his story. When he had finished he said,

'Simon, you have been living outside yourself. You have been playing a part written for another. A model is not a mould into which we pour ourselves, but a spur to help us to be true to what is within us, to what is given to us and only to us.

'The most important task in life is to become ourselves. Unless we become ourselves, no growth, no happiness, no holiness is possible. But when we become ourselves, then everything about us becomes real and true. Francis became a saint, not by becoming someone else, but by becoming his true and full self.

'Simon, when you come before the Lord on the day of judge-

ment, he won't ask you, Why didn't you become Francis of Assisi?
No, he will ask you, Why didn't you become Simon?'

The Leave-taking

Before taking leave of us the Master spoke more than once about his
impending departure. In doing so he used a strange phrase. He said,
'It is for your own good that I leave.' Frankly, I found it incomprehensible. I saw his leaving as an unmitigated disaster, and the mere
thought of it filled me with sorrow.

Then one evening in late November we were walking along a certain road. The sky was clear and the air crisp. The sun was going
down behind us, filling the landscape with its golden light as it did
so. Yet, in spite of the gold the sun radiated, the world had an over-
familiar, worn-out and rusty appearance. Autumn had plundered it
of all the fruits of summer.

At a certain point the Master said, 'Look at the moon.' I quickly
scanned the sky but failed to locate it. I looked again, this time
slowly and searchingly. Still nothing. Finally, I spotted it high to my
right. Though it was almost full, it was so pale and weak as to be
practically invisible. Having located it, I continued to gaze at it for
some moments. It didn't appear to be contributing anything whatso-
ever to the earth.

Meanwhile the sun went on with its leave-taking. It seemed to be
taking the whole world with it. However, as it withdrew I noticed a
curious and beautiful thing. The lower the sun dipped in the sky, the
brighter the moon became. By the time the sun had finally departed
the scene, the moon had undergone a complete transformation. It
was now, far and away, the brightest object in the evening sky.

Of course, even at its zenith, it could not compare with the sun.
Yet its silvery light was not only adequate to see by, but cast an enchantment over everything. As I looked around me I noticed to my

surprise and delight that the old world had not only been completely restored to us, but had been made new, bright and exciting.

It was only when the sun had withdrawn that I could see what the moon was contributing. I was aware, of course, that it only reflected the light of the sun, now hidden from us. It still needed the sun, but the sun also needed it to reflect its light on the earth. As I was thinking about this, the Master spoke again.

'That's what love does,' he said. He gave me time to think about this remark before going on. When he continued he said, 'Loving at times means distancing oneself from those we love. This leaves them free to develop in their own way as well as to receive from others. They come to realise that they have a unique contribution to make, and are given an opportunity to make it.'

This made immediate sense to me. How often we do the exact opposite, I thought. We hug the limelight. We want to be present all the time. We do not know when or how to withdraw. Thus in a thoughtless and selfish way we dominate others. We keep them in the shadows, stifling their development. There is, however, an art in withdrawing. We have to withdraw in such a way that we do not give them the impression that we are abandoning them.

As we walked on in silence I gazed once more at the moon. It was now shining so brightly that you would think it had a secret source of light within itself. Under its quiet light all sorts of little creatures who could not endure the heat of the sun had ventured out into the open. The night was alive with rustlings.

All of a sudden I no longer felt so bad about the Master's imminent departure.

Biblical Index

Lectionary Index